THE AK47
CHRIS McNAB

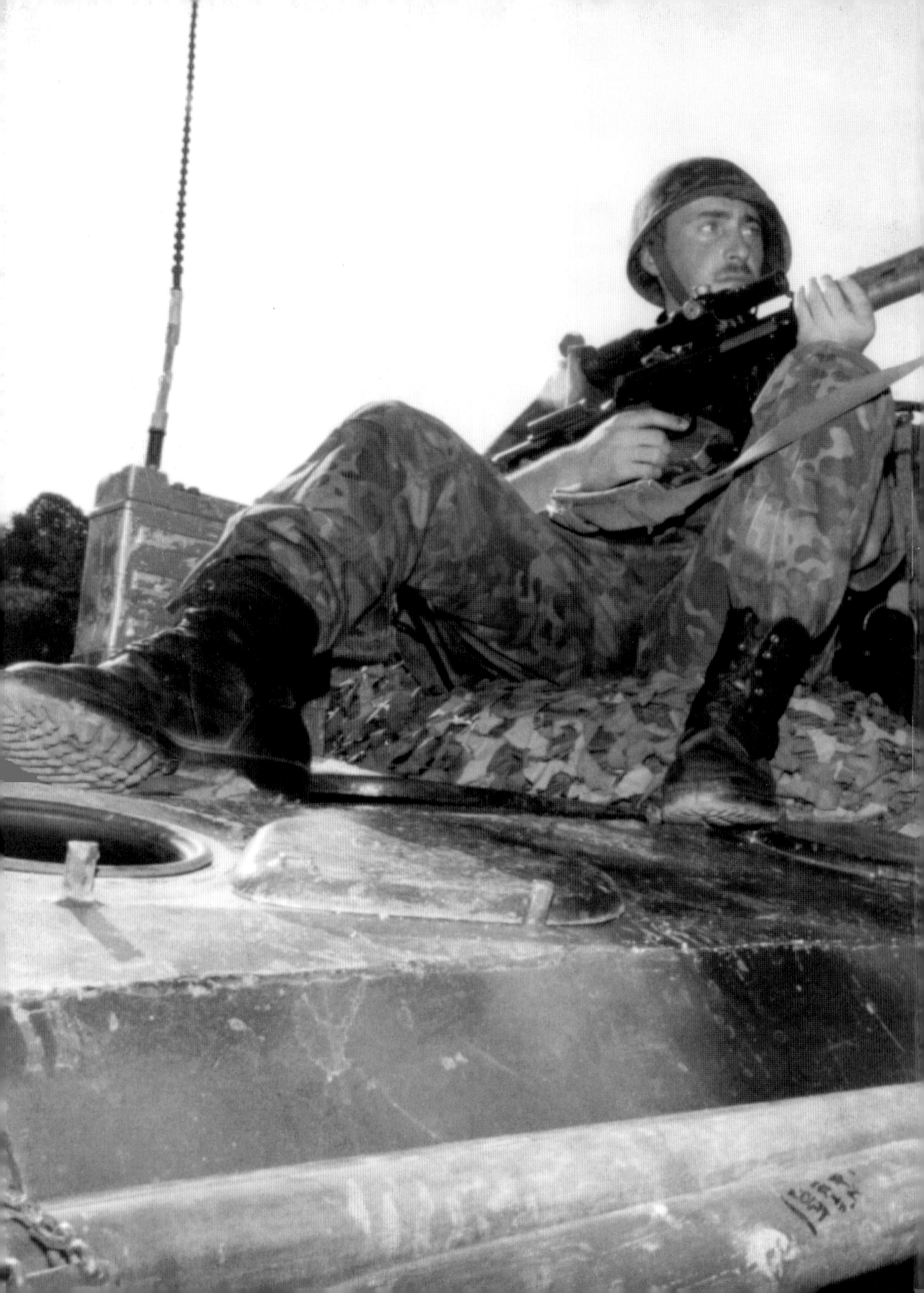

THE AK47

CHRIS McNAB

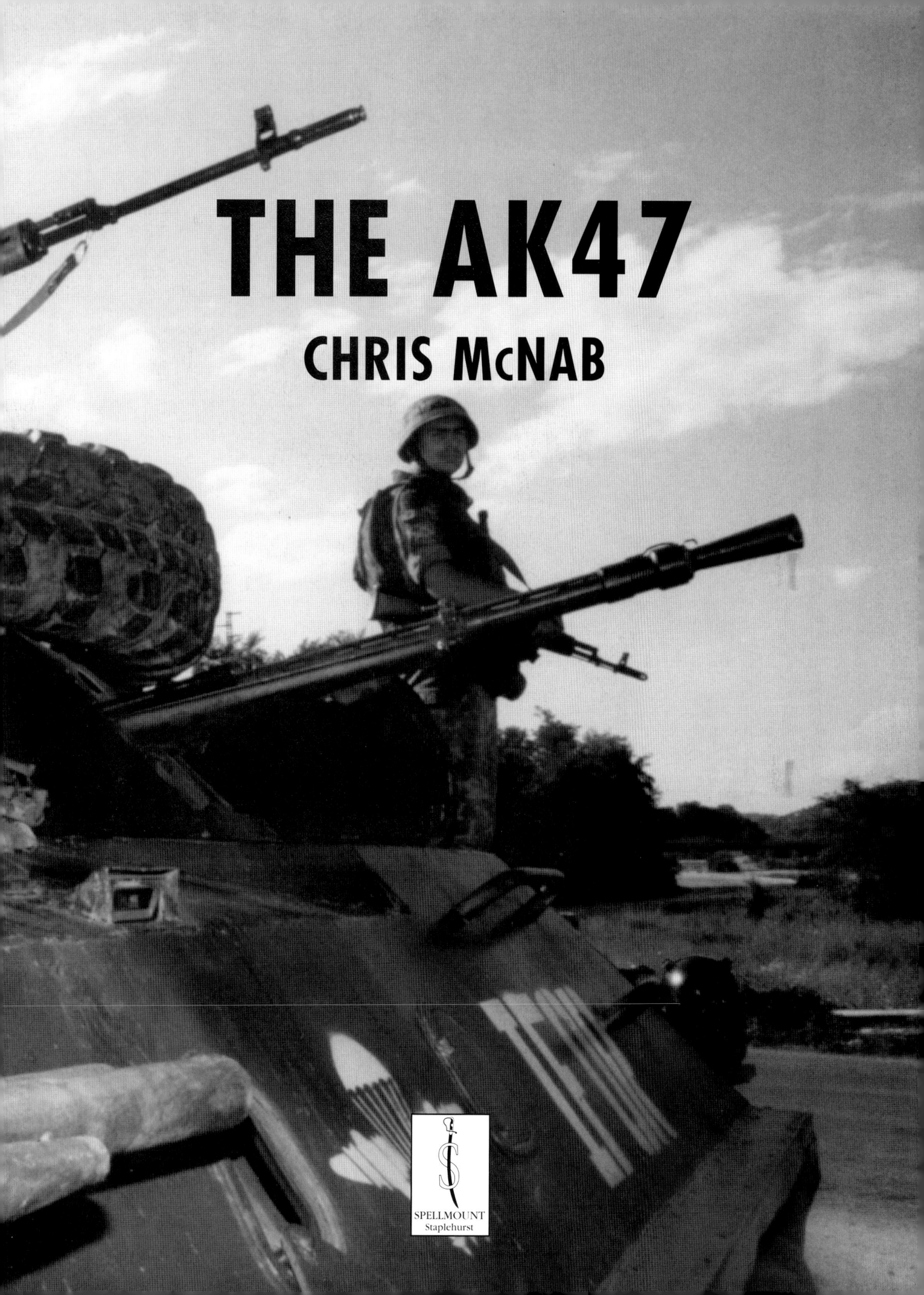

SPELLMOUNT
Staplehurst

British Library Cataloguing in Publication Data:
A catalogue record for this book is available
from the British Library

Copyright © Amber Books Ltd 2001

ISBN 1-86227-116-X

First published in the UK in 2001 by
Spellmount Ltd
The Old Rectory
Staplehurst
Kent TN12 0AZ

Tel: 01580 893730
Fax: 01580 893731
E-mail: enquiries@spellmount.com
Website: www.spellmount.com

1 3 5 7 9 8 6 4 2

All rights reserved. No part of this publication may be
reproduced, stored in a retrieval system or transmitted in
any form or by any means, electronic, mechanical,
photocopying, recording or otherwise,
without prior permission in writing from
Spellmount Limited, Publishers.

Editorial and design: Amber Books Ltd
Bradley's Close, 74-77 White Lion Street,
London N1 9PF

Project Editor: Charles Catton/Chris Stone
Design: Hawes Design

Printed and bound in The Slovak Republic

Pages 2-3: A Russian soldier armed with a Dragunov SVD sniper rifle, a sophisticated AK variant with a killing range of more than 800 metres.

CONTENTS

CHAPTER 1
The Making of the AK47   6

CHAPTER 2
Design and Development   20

CHAPTER 3
Usage and Training   34

CHAPTER 4
Deployment and Battle   48

CHAPTER 5
AK Variants   68

Appendices   92

Index   95

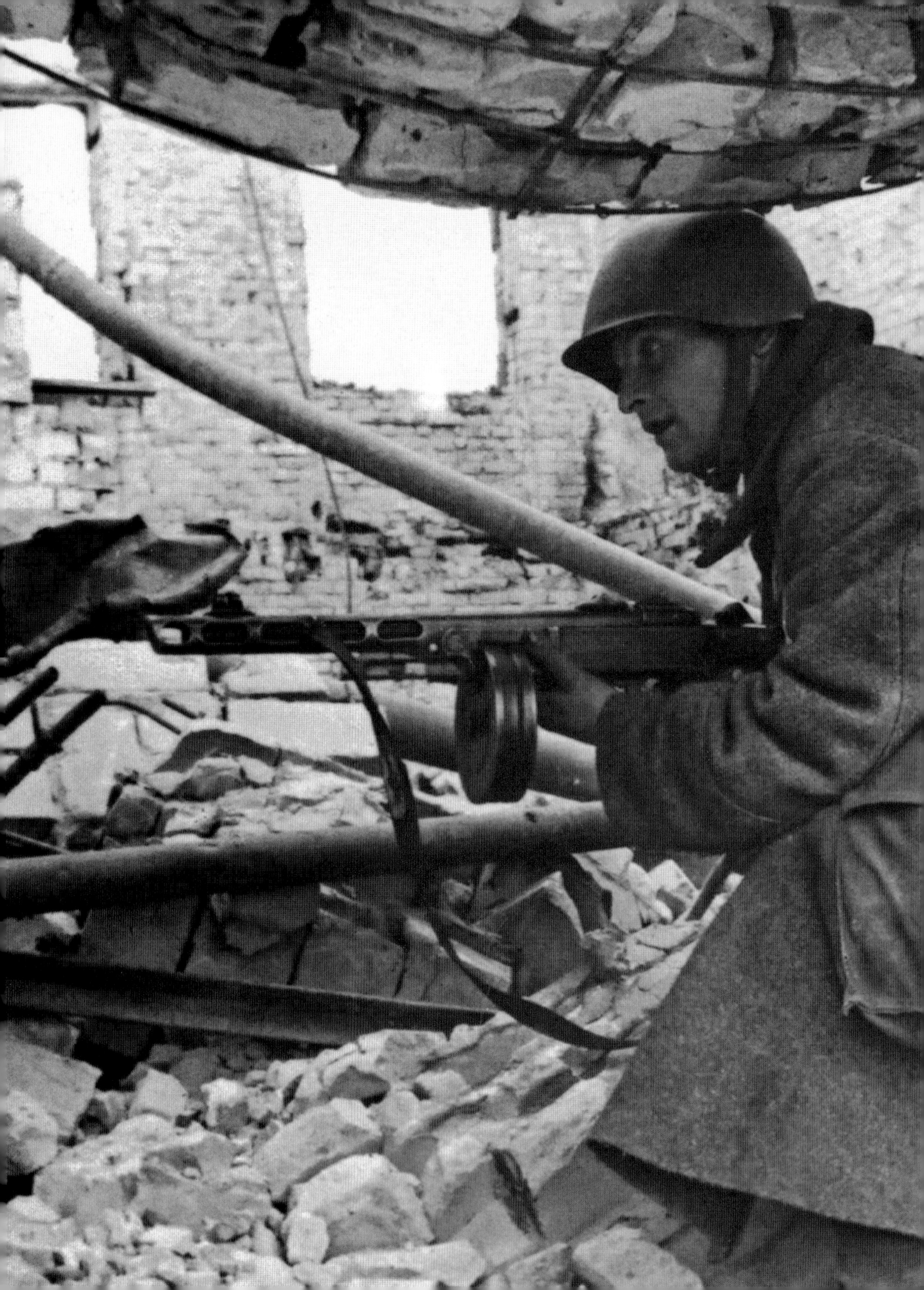

CHAPTER 1

The Making of the AK47

Few weapons have had a greater impact on the history of men-at-arms, and indeed history in general, as Kalashnikov's AK47.

Its acceptance as the standard assault rifle for Soviet forces in 1949 set in train the production of an astonishing 80 million AK47s or immediate variants – 80 million hard-hitting medium-range killing tools which were easy to operate, rarely failed, and simple to manufacture. The AK47 became a truly global presence in military, insurgent and civilian hands. It was almost as much of an icon of the Soviet ideology as the hammer and sickle. It has killed and injured in almost every conflict since the early 1950s, and modern variations and scattered, unaccounted stocks ensure that it will continue to do so for many years to come. The historical consequences of giving so much of the world such heavy personal firepower is still being evaluated.

THE INTERMEDIATE CARTRIDGE

The AK47 was not designed upon impulse or simple inspiration. In fact, it emerged out of Soviet developments in ammunition technology in the early 1940s. During this period, changes in tactical thinking about small arms led Soviet military authorities to commission the design of a new 'intermediate' cartridge, a round somewhere between a rifle cartridge and a pistol cartridge in terms of power and performance. It was to accommodate this new cartridge that the AK was designed. Yet the story of how this intermediate round came into being is somewhat clouded in confusion, and needs clarification.

At the beginning of World War II, military small-arms ammunition had separated into two essential formats. At the smaller end of the scale were pistol-calibre rounds. These ranged between about 5mm (0.19in) and 15mm (0.59in) and had a case length generally between 8mm (0.31in) and 13mm (0.51in). Performance varied dramatically, but muzzle velocity tended to gather around 250–350mps (820–1148fps) and a practical range about 20–30m (65–98ft). Pistol-calibre rounds

Left: A Russian infantryman stalks warily through the rubble of Stalingrad carrying his PPSh41. By the early 1940s, Soviet authorities had already begun the quest for the perfect infantry weapon.

were used, naturally, in handguns but also in submachine guns. This latter application originated in the combat experience of World War I. Trench warfare sat at odds with the supposed advantages of the standard long-range infantry rifle. A 1000m + range was superfluous when trench systems were often little more than 100m (328ft) apart, plus the blast of the cartridge acted as a valuable locator signature for the enemy in low-light conditions. The powerful round also made the rifle much more difficult to handle accurately in unskilled hands, consequently pushing up training times which were constrained once mass conscription came into play. The advantages of long-range firepower were particularly undone in actions during which enemy trenches were entered. World War I trench systems were kinked or even crenellated every 5–10m (16–33ft) or so, and in a confused trench battle a high-power rifle round would have little currency with its excessive penetrative power (which would endanger one's own comrades) and the need to manually load each cartridge by physically working the bolt. Furthermore, the great length of most of the rifles made them incredibly difficult to wield in narrow trenches, some of which could be narrower than the length of the rifles. Finally, the limits of the magazine capacity and the method of reloading meant that in vigorous combat a magazine could be quickly expended and difficult to replenish.

Below: The contrast between full power and intermediate ammunition is clearly shown in this representative spread of post-war ammunition types. From left to right: 7.62mm M1891; 7.62mm NATO; 7.92mm MR43; 7.62mm M43.

The experience of trench warfare led many military authorities to re-evaluate the reality of combat distances. In close trench warfare, the distances were generally well under 15.24m (50ft) but even across open land 300m (984ft) usually set the visual and practical limit of effective fire. For the most compact styles of warfare emerged the submachine gun, weapons like the Bergmann MP18 leading the way. Short and easily wielded, firing a controllable pistol-calibre cartridge, capable of full automatic modes of fire, and usually featuring a large magazine capacity, the submachine gun was an ideal close-quarters weapon and went on to have a long history which is far from over.

While pistol-calibre cartridges inhabited the close-quarters spectrum of combat, the psychological commitment to long-range rifle marksmanship and the ubiquitous presence of the bolt-action rifle meant that full-power cartridges were still the dominant currency at the beginning of World War II. While actual calibre varied between about 6mm (0.23in) and 8mm (0.31in), cartridge length rarely reached below 50mm (1.96in). For example, the Mauser Gewehr 98 fired a 7.92 x 57mm cartridge which weighed 11.52gm (0.025lb) and (when using German Ball SmE Lang cartridges) propelled the bullet at 896mps (2939fps) to a range of well over 1000m (3280ft). The 1000m+ range of the Gewehr 98 was a typical aspiration of military rifles at the time, and was felt to be vital for the soldier's command of the open battlefield. A design corollary of this was a long barrel, necessary to give the accuracy for hitting targets at the limit of visual range, and thus extensive overall gun dimensions and weight. Barrel length on

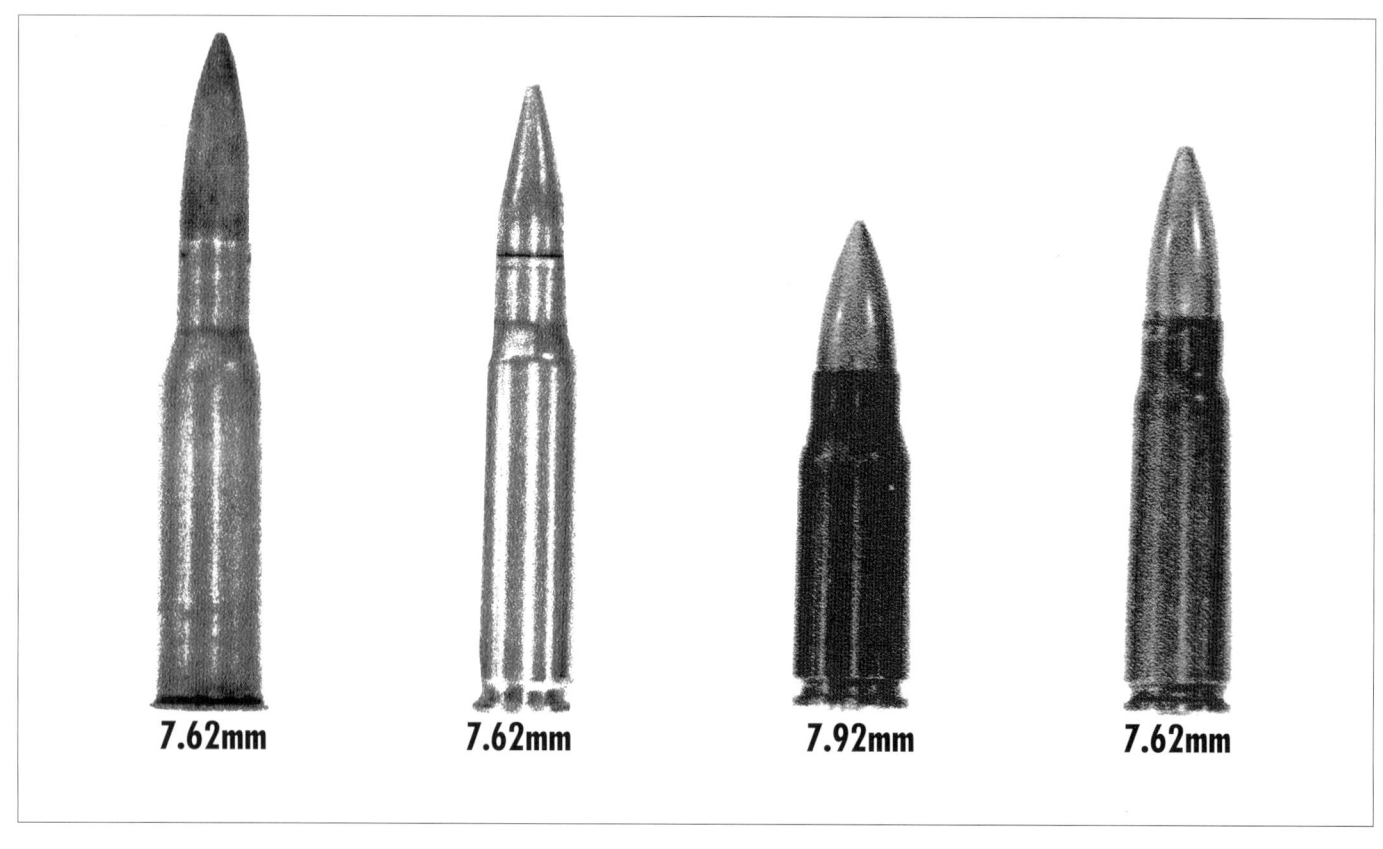

7.62mm   **7.62mm**   **7.92mm**   **7.62mm**

Above: A medic of the Red Guard struggles through the snow of the Eastern Front, 1942. On his back he carries a mix of old and new: three 7.62mm Mosin-Nagant rifles and a Tokarev automatic rifle.

the Russian M1891 reached 800mm (31.5in), this giving a gun length of 1240mm (48.82in) and an overall weight of 4.35kg (9.59lb). Carbine versions of many rifles were developed as attempts to control gun specifications, but even amongst these barrel length generally stayed above the 600mm (23.6in) mark (any shorter and the muzzle blast from the cartridge started to become an obstacle to efficient use).

In the early decades of the Soviet Union, one rifle cartridge was dominant – the 7.62 x 54R Mosin-Nagant. This venerable round entered service in the aforementioned M1891 designed by Emil and Leon Nagant and Captain S.I. Mosin of the Russian Imperial Artillery. The round had a case length of 53.60mm (2.1in) and, depending on the rifle, it could achieve a muzzle velocity of around 870mps (2854fps) and a range in excess of 1000m (3280ft). While the M1891 round was perfectly compatible with the times when it was first produced, its awkward rimmed shape and inconsistent manufacture started to cause problems with the experimentations in self-loading rifles that gathered apace from the late 1800s.

By the beginning of World War II many nations had developed self-loading rifles with varying degrees of success. At one end of the scale was Mauser's disastrous series of recoil-operated weapons, while at the other was the gas-operated US M1 Garand which would go on to be the standard rifle of US forces until the late 1950s. What unites the various models produced was their usage of standard rifle cartridges, despite the fact that the sheer power of previously bolt-action rounds placed severe burdens on the pistons, bolts and breech blocks of self-loading weapons. Such a situation was equally true in the Soviet Union. Automatic rifle development there began with Federov (who will be discussed later) in 1916, but by the 1920s and 30s Soviet authorities were eager enough for the new format to commission numerous competitions to design automatic rifles.

The participants in these competitions formed a roll-call of some of Soviet history's most esteemed designers – Degtyarev, Simonov, Tokarev, Federov. Between 1930 and 1940 the dominant names in self-loading design were the first three of this list. Yet their creative handling of self-loading rifles was curtailed by the standardisation of the 7.62 x 54R round. During

THE AK47

Above: Soviet troops relax in the aftermath of the war's end. The PPSh41 weapons would serve for years to come, yet their battlefield rationale was challenged by the introduction of the assault rifle.

the weapons trials of 1938, the competitive criteria were given direct from Commander First Class Boris Shapashnikov at Red Army general headquarters. These criteria included demands for durability, ease of use, simplicity of manufacture, and that all guns submitted had to take the M1891 round. The three main competitors – Fedor Tokarev, Sergey Simonov and Nikolay Rukavashnikov – all submitted gas-operated, fixed-barrel weapons and, after all submissions were initially rejected in the tests of 25 August–03 September, in the final trials in November 1938 Tokarev won with the SVT38 design (despite the fact that history has shown Simonov's design to be better).

The SVT38 and later SVT40 were perfectly serviceable rifles, but many of the problems which did occur in their use were down to the ammunition. Rimmed rounds made for an unpredictable feed from a box magazine, and the recoil force generated by a full-power round placed extreme wear on the self-loading mechanisms. Furthermore, full-automatic fire was not practical owing to violent muzzle climb and poor accuracy resulted from excessive recoil and muzzle blast. These problems coincided with a general rethink concerning the value of the full-power round during the inter-war years within and outside the USSR. In the 1930s, Germany had conducted studies into the fighting ranges of World War I, and concluded that 500m (1640ft) was the upper limit at which most combat generally occurred. Above that visual contact was limited and, unless sniping, accurate fire was extremely difficult. Since the pistol cartridge only offered an alternative at the lower ends of range and power, what was required was a round that inhabited the middle ground between long-range rifle and short-range pistol cartridges. Once this was found a barrier was broken and the modern assault rifle could be born.

Pre-revolutionary Russia unwittingly played host to just such a development in 1916. In that year, Vladimir Grigorevich Fedorov, an arms designer in the pay of the Tsarist court, designed the 6.5mm Fedorov 'Avtomat'. The significance of the Avtomat lies not so much in its design –

Left: These German mountain troops might appreciate the 1000m + range of their Mausers in mountain settings, but in urban environments like this the range would have been generally impractical.

THE AK47

PPSh41

Calibre:	7.62 x 25mm Soviet
Length:	838mm (33in)
Weight:	3.64kg (8lb)
Feed:	35-round detachable box magazine
System of operation:	Blow-back
Rate of fire (cyclic):	900rpm
Muzzle velocity:	500mps (1640fps)

THE MAKING OF THE AK47

Left: Russian guerrilla fighters train with their Mosin-Nagant rifles. The powerful round fired by these weapons meant that effective training times had to be high or battlefield accuracy would be poor.

short-recoil operation feeding off a curved 25-round magazine – as in its cartridge. Rather than opting for the powerful standard 7.62 x 54R rifle cartridge Federov chose the 'intermediate' 6.5mm Meiji 30 cartridge used in Japanese rifles. The selection was made because Federov found that the full-power rifle rounds imposed too high a level of wear and tear on his design, and required such durable bolts, pistons and breech blocks that the gun became excessively heavy.

Federov's Avtomat was in many senses the world's first assault rifle – though as Ian Hogg has rightly pointed out this was more a case of accident than intention. It is very plausible that Federov's selection of cartridge had more of an influence behind the Soviet military's development of the M43 intermediate round (the round used by the AK47) in the 1940s than the German 7.92 x 33mm Kurz to which the inspiration is commonly ascribed. It is equally clear that Federov's influential arms manuals went on to have an influence on the young Kalashnikov when he was designing the AK gun. However, the particular junction of history in which Federov was working greatly limited the influence of the Avtomat. Tedious post-revolutionary bureaucracy and labour regulations placed heavy chains on the Avtomat's production. Federov even spent time in prison because of his beliefs

Above: The MP44 has been termed 'the father of all assault rifles'. This honour has some legitimacy, and the appearance of the MP44 has instant suggestions of the final design layout of the AK47.

Above: Soviet troops advance west on a T34. Kalashnikov was a tank man until he was injured. However, his convalescence allowed him to talk to infantry and discuss their experience of small arms.

in the value of master labourers which sat at odds with communist egalitarianism. Production never exceeded 50 rifles per month and the Avtomat's design was effectively undone when the authorities re-imposed the old 7.62mm round – breakdowns and stoppages thus became common and production ceased in 1924.

Because of such bureaucratic fetters, the value of Federov's gun was lost to the Soviet Union and Germany took the lead in cartridge development. The first intermediate round specifically produced was the 7.75mm (later 7.62mm) M35 by Gustave Genschow and Co. Unlike the 7.92mm Mauser's case length of 56.8mm (2.23in), the M35 had a case length of only 39.5mm (1.55in) and a muzzle velocity of 700mps (2296fps) rather than 850mps (2788fps) of the Mauser. The M35 required a gun to fit around it, and this was provided in the MKb35 designed by Heinrich Vollmer. The MKb35 (standing for Maschinekarabine 35) was little more than experimental, its extreme cost of manufacture (about 4000 Reichsmarks) and erratic performance meaning that it and the M35 round soon disappeared from the German arsenal once war began.

The same cannot be said for the 7.92 x 33mm Kurz round which followed it, designed by Polte Werke of Magdeburg. This took the standard Mauser cartridge and reduced its length to 33mm (1.3in) and utilised 31 grains of propellant. Muzzle velocity was around 700mps (2296fps). The Kurz round was developed following the lessons of combat distance encountered in the early campaigns on the Eastern Front, and it went on to be used in several purpose-designed carbines and assault rifles. The most famous of these was the MP43 (alternatively designated MP44 or StG44 in the year following its entry). This weapon – ultra-modern for the time and probably the first genuine assault rifle – embodied all the new philosophies of combat range and bears a more than passing resemblance to the weapon which is the subject of this book. What is significant is that around the time of the development of the Kurz round and simultaneously with the problems encountered in the SVT38/40, Stalin and his Defence Committee gave the green light for the development of an intermediate cartridge which could be used in a

THE MAKING OF THE AK47

new type of assault rifle. The criteria laid down for the new round included its calibre - 7.62mm - its optimal killing range - 300-400m (984-1312ft) and the gun barrel length to be used - 500-520mm (19.6-20.5in). In 1943, the winner was announced. Engineers N.M Elizarov and B.V. Semin produced the 7.62 x 39mm Model 1943 cartridge - or M43. It fulfilled all the criteria imposed by the Soviet high command. Today, controversy still reigns over where inspiration for the round came from. Popularly it is laid at the door of the German Kurz round, and it is admitted that the Soviets were impressed by the round's performance when encountered through the MP44 on the Eastern Front. Yet the M43's dimensions are far more similar to the German M35, and indeed Soviet designers had access to the round after a small supply of MKb35s were captured on the Eastern Front. Tracing the exact derivation of the M43 is difficult. More likely is that all the tendencies towards intermediate-power rounds fed into the M43 design process, including Federov's experiments in 1916 (Federov wrote many influential weapon design manuals of which Semin and Elizarov would have been almost certainly aware).

Whatever the origin, by 1943 the Soviet Union had their new assault rifle round but, ironically, no gun in which to use it. It is at this point that the figure of Mikhail Timofeyevich Kalashnikov steps out of the shadows.

KALASHNIKOV – THE EARLY YEARS

M.T. Kalashnikov was born on 10 November 1919 in the village of Kurya, Altai territory, Kazakhstan. His background was rural and inauspicious, yet he soon showed himself as an academically bright child. In 1936 he graduated from what is known as 'ten year school' - equivalent to US High School - and subsequently entered work as an apprentice and technical clerk at the Turkestan-Siberia railroad's Matai depot based at Alma-Ata. There he achieved the position of technical secretary, before the Red Army's recruitment drive in the late 1930s (often focused at the technically talented railroad personnel) drew him into military service.

Kalashnikov entered the army in 1938, and the logistics and equipment of the army environment only served to foster his engineering vision. He trained as an armourer after basic training before going on to complete courses in tank driving and tank engineering. During this early period in the military, Kalashnikov produced several inventions which entered service with the Red Army. These included: a tank-gun shot counter, a modification to the TT pistol for use through tank observation slits, improvements to tank-track assembly, and also a tank-engine monitoring device which checked levels of power and fuel consumption. It was this latter invention which sent Kalashnikov to Leningrad to supervise the production of his gauges in a factory there.

In 1941, Germany launched Operation Barbarossa, a surge into the Russian motherland that required the mobilisation of almost every active Russian male, including the young Kalashnikov. As a trained tank driver and by now the rank of Senior Sergeant, Kalashnikov found himself as a front-line T34 tank commander in the First Tank Army. In October of that year, Kalashnikov was engaged in heavy fighting around Bryansk when a German shell hit his tank and severely wounded him in the shoulder. He was immediately sent to military hospital which was followed by a six-month period of convalescence.

It is a matter of endless speculation whether the world would now be in possession of the AK rifles had Kalashnikov not been wounded. For it was in hospital at Kazan that Kalashnikov began talking with the wounded infantry around him. Through their accounts of battle Kalashnikov became aware of the disparities of firepower which existed between German and Russian forces, particularly in terms of the lack of submachine guns available to most troops. Kalashnikov seemed to sense a challenge and need. His hospital bed and ward became the site of intense study into all

Below: The PPS43 was one of the best submachine guns of the war. Kalashnikov attempted a similar design in 1942/3, but the market was already cornered by the PPS43 and the excellent PPSh41.

THE AK47

Above: The Simonov SKS was the first Soviet weapon to fire the new 7.62mm M43 cartridge. Though it was eventually superseded by the AK47, it was a successful gun in its own right.

existing small arms design. Paper started to fill up with Kalashnikov's own ideas for new guns and design modifications, and his interest was led down the route of designing a new submachine gun to rival the German MP38/40.

Kalashnikov's wounds had been serious enough for him to qualify for six months service/convalescence leave in the railroad depots back at Alma-Ata (he also left hospital with an award of the Order of the Red Star). The destination of his leave was fortuitous, as the Matai depot's workshops gave him the requisite means to experiment with his gun designs. In addition, he could also access the support of the many talented engineers working at the site.

As a young engineer with no track record of firearm design, Kalashnikov must have seemed to possess impractical ambition. Submachine-gun design had been attempted with varying levels of success by many of the great Soviet gun designers, including V.A. Degtyarev (PPD34/38/40) and Georgi Shpagin who produced the superb and legendary PPSh41. In 1942 a competition was issued to design a new submachine gun for Soviet forces. Though the competition included both Degtyarev and Shpagin, Kalashnikov precociously entered. His first idea was for a gun using the 7.62mm TT pistol cartridge (the standard submachine gun round used at the time) in a delayed-blowback configuration and fed from a staggered-row 30-round detachable box magazine. Kalashnikov was helped in his task by friend and machinist Zhenya Kravchenko, and consequently he was able to build a first prototype of his gun.

Kalashnikov's first submachine gun did not gain acceptance, but it did awaken influential people to this potential rising star. The weapon was evaluated by the Kazakh Central Committee of the Communist Party, the Secretary of which saw to it that Kalashnikov was transferred to the much-improved working conditions of the Ordzhonikidze Moscow Aviation Institute (the Institute had been transferred to Alma-Ata in the face of the German advance.) Here it was that Kalashnikov built a full prototype of his submachine gun. Testing followed, and when Kalashnikov was satisfied he submitted the gun to the Dzerhinsky Artillery Academy in Samarkand for evaluation. Kalashnikov's weapon was closely inspected by experts, including General Anatoly Arkadaevich Blagonravov who held the Chair of Infantry Weapons at the Academy. Blagonravov rejected the weapon on several grounds including over-complexity, yet he recognised that the design had come from a talented individual made more impressive by his self-taught origins. To encourage this talent, Blagonravov enabled Kalashnikov to receive formal education and training in weaponry design, even though by now Aleksei Sudaeyev had won the submachine-gun competition with his excellent PPS-43 weapon.

From 1942 Kalashnikov became a technician at the Central Research Small Arms Range of the Main Ordnance Directorate of the Red Army at Ensk. These were to prove fruitful and informative years. He made physical modifications to Goryunov's machine guns, work which gained him two 'Author's Certificates' – similar to patents but purged of any supposed elitist non-communist connotations. Vitally, Kalashnikov also met the great Soviet gun designers, including Degtyarev, Simonov and Sudaeyev, and this almost certainly made Kalashnikov gain in confidence through admission to the inner circle of Soviet gun design.

That confidence was soon to be tested. In 1944 Kalashnikov was given a stock of the new M43 intermediate cartridges. From receipt of this stock, Kalashnikov turned his attention away from submachine-gun design, and focused on the automatic rifle as the way forward.

THE ROUTE TO THE AK47

The release of the M43 cartridge prompted an explosion in creative efforts from Soviet gun designers – particularly from

THE MAKING OF THE AK47

the minds of Sudaeyev, Simonov and the young Kalashnikov. The first of these designers actually to produce a weapon for the M43 was Sudaeyev. His conception was a blow-back operated avtomat released for testing in January 1944. The design was unconvincing. Blow-back was ill-suited to the demands of the rifle-calibre cartridges (blow-back tends to be confined to pistol and submachine-gun design) and it was an unwieldy instrument. A second design from Sudaeyev was released with the more reasonable rotating-bolt configuration, but it did not solve the weight problem of the earlier weapon and thus Sudaeyev was essentially removed from the M43 race.

Meanwhile, Kalashnikov had arrived at his first design. Through a furious process of construction, testing and continual amendments Kalashnikov produced a self-loading carbine

Right: Mr Kalashnikov (pictured with the weapon that made him famous) was highly decorated by the Soviet state throughout his lifetime for his incredible contribution to the history of men at arms.

THE SVT38

The Samozaryadnaya Vintovka obr 1938, or SVT38, was one in a long line of automatic rifles designed by Feydor Vassilivich Tokarev from the late 1920s. Tokarev had previously been beaten in competition to design a Soviet production assault rifle in 1930 by Simonov's AVS. Yet the AVS did not live up to all expectations – there were problems with dirt intrusion and locking could be inefficient – and less than 66,000 were made. Thus in 1938 competition was once again opened for an issue self-loading rifle. After more than a year of testing, Tokarev's SVT38 was accepted and put into production. The decision to replace the AVS with the Tokarev remains controversial to this day, but the Tokarev on the whole presents a more simple and reliable weapon.

The SVT38 is a gas-operated rifle. Its locking action is of a distinctive tipping-block type: a moving block is cammed downwards into a recess in the receiver floor to lock the bolt and carrier in place, this block being released by the backward motion of the bolt-carrier upon recoil. The whole appearance was long and slender, though this construction was found to be somewhat fragile when knocked around during combat. The two-piece stock and fore-end led into a metal extension over the barrel that was drilled through with ventilation holes to aid cooling. Another distinctive feature is a six-baffle muzzle brake – a requisite fitting when firing the 7.62 x 54R cartridge – though this was simplified in the early 1940s to only two baffles. Feed is from a 10-round detachable box magazine.

analysed, the conclusion being that the SVT38 was sound in principle but lacked the durability required of a combat weapon. Improvements were made, resulting in the SVT40, though most of the improvements were focused into production techniques rather than firing properties. Visually there are few features which separate the two weapons. The SVT40 had its cleaning rod situated under the barrel – the SVT38 had its against the side of the forestock. The SVT40's muzzle brake also came in six- or two-baffle versions. Everything else – weight, length, power – stayed almost exactly the same. Variants of the SVT40, however, were the AVT40 which was the same rifle modified to be capable of automatic fire, and a carbine version. Little is known about the use of these latter weapons as production of them appears to have been limited. Based on field reports the SVT40 was a competent firearm, but it did not survive after the war as the shift to assault rifle design was pursued.

Specifications

Country of Origin:	USSR/Russia
Calibre:	7.62 x 52R
Length:	1222mm (48.11in)
Weight:	3.95kg (8.71lb)
Barrel:	610mm (24in), 4 grooves, rh
Feed/Magazine capacity:	10-round detachable box magazine
Operation:	Gas
Cyclic rate of fire:	Semi-automatic
Muzzle Velocity:	840mps (2755fps)

THE AK47

in 1944. This was gas-operated with the gas piston situated below the barrel and it utilised a rotating bolt. Feed was from a ten-round charger-loaded integral magazine and the ejection functioned upon a spring-loaded deflector sited on the upper right part of the bolt. Kalashnikov was not to make his mark with this experimental carbine, but certain features allude to the forthcoming AK47 design. Chief amongst these was an increased rotation of the bolt when compared with other similar weapons, something which greatly assisted the reliability for which the AK47 would become famous.

The experimental carbine, however, was eclipsed by another carbine design from the hands of Simonov. The Simonov SKS was to be the first gun adopted for the M43. Unlike Kalashnikov's design, the SKS worked through a tipping-bolt system of locking, a system which Simonov actually derived from the PTRS anti-tank rifle. There was much positive to be said about the SKS. Combat trials on the Byelorussian Front showed that it was easy to use and maintain, its charger system allowed full clips or single rounds to be loaded into the magazine, and it was both controllable and accurate. Such qualities ensured a good future for the SKS. Following its adoption in the Soviet Union as the SKS-45, Simonov's rifle not only entered standard army service but also went on to be produced as variations by Yugoslavia, North Korea, China, and East Germany. Yet the SKS was not without its faults. It was vulnerable to dust and dirt, and both feed and extraction could cause problems. Nevertheless, with the market for carbines effectively cornered by Simonov, Kalashnikov was led to abandon his carbine experiments. The market for rifles, however, was another matter.

Kalashnikov himself has documented some of the mental challenges that the design of a new avtomat would pose.

'It still seemed presumptuous in my mind, and I asked myself: "experienced designers and gunsmiths are already working on this, will you be able to say a new word, to make a better system?" But the knowledge that many of my "threatening rivals" had sometimes felt the same way, let me begin on my path. And my audacity increased ... again on sheets of drawing paper more and more new variants of new designs appeared.'

Despite the sense of creative isolation that comes through here, Kalashnikov did not tackle the avtomat project on his own. He worked closely with a team of technical specialists in an extraordinarily energetic period of design. Finally, by early 1946 drawings of a new gas-operated, rotating-bolt assault rifle were ready for submission to the GRAU (the Soviet artillery commission) in Moscow. Response was favourable, and Kalashnikov received approval and more assistance to take his experimental design to the working model stage.

The prototype Kalashnikov produced is instantly recognisable as the forerunner of the AK47, though the general appearance is far more box-like and crude than what was to follow. The receiver is very flat and less angled at the rear with the selector lever positioned on the left behind the trigger group (the production AK47 has the selector on the right), and it has the visual hallmarks of a stamped-metal construction. The buttstock is fitted onto this receiver by way of two metal extensions. A second prototype is also in

Left: A corporal of the Soviet infantry in typical dress. His firearm is the Tokarev SVT40, a weapon which gave credible performance but which was later dwarfed by the assault rifle format.

THE MAKING OF THE AK47

evidence, this gun featuring a 450mm (17.7in) barrel as opposed to the first prototype's 397mm (15.6in) barrel. These guns were labelled AK#1 and AK#2 and their configurations were recognisably those of the AK47.

In 1947, after yet another rigorous period of redesign and re-evaluation, Kalashnikov arrived at a new model of his rifle which he labelled the AK47. This was an attempt by Kalashnikov and his assistant Aleksandr Zaytsev to make the AK the final word in reliability and practicality (other guns in the trials submitted by Demetev and Bulkin had jammed and were thus rejected). Extensive work was put into the breechblock mechanism which Kalashnikov admits he 'borrowed' from his 'abortive carbine' of a few years earlier. He also refined his submission procedure, especially in the presentation of technical data, and handed the AK47 over for testing.

The results were stunning. In 1949, an ebullient Engineer-Colonel Vladimir Sergeyevich Demin announced to a shocked Kalashnikov that his Avtomat Kalashnikova obrazets 1947g had been accepted as a standard Red Army weapon. The trials had revealed a weapon of amazing reliability, the capacity for absorbing all manner of hard knocks and harsh environments, and which was capable of doing its grim business with efficiency and operative ease. From this point, the AK47 began its journey towards the legendary status it holds today. The exact mechanical properties which enabled it to make this journey is the subject of the next chapter.

Below: Soviet snipers in action with Tokarev rifles. Because the Tokarev retained the full power 7.62 x 52R round it maintained an effective medium-range sniper utility of over 500m (1640ft).

THE SVT40

The SVT40 was the replacement for the SVT38, and it stepped into the latter's shoes as an attempt to make the Tokarev guns more solid and serviceable in combat conditions. Visually the distinctions were fairly undramatic between the two guns. The SVT40 had its cleaning rod situated under the barrel rather than against the side of the forestock as it was in the SVT38. The SVT40's muzzle brake also came in six- or two-baffle versions. Everything else – weight, length, power – stayed almost exactly the same. Variants of the SVT40, however, were the AVT40 which was the same rifle modified to be capable of automatic fire, and the SVT40, a carbine version. Little is known about the use of these weapons as production of them appears to have been limited.

Specifications

Country of Origin:	USSR/Russia
Calibre:	7.62 x 52R
Length:	1226mm (48.27in)
Weight:	3.90kg (8.6lb)
Barrel:	610mm (24in), 4 grooves, rh
Feed/Magazine capacity:	10-round detachable box magazine
Operation:	Gas
Cyclic rate of fire:	Semi-automatic
Muzzle Velocity:	840mps (2755fps)
Effective Range:	500m (1640ft) +

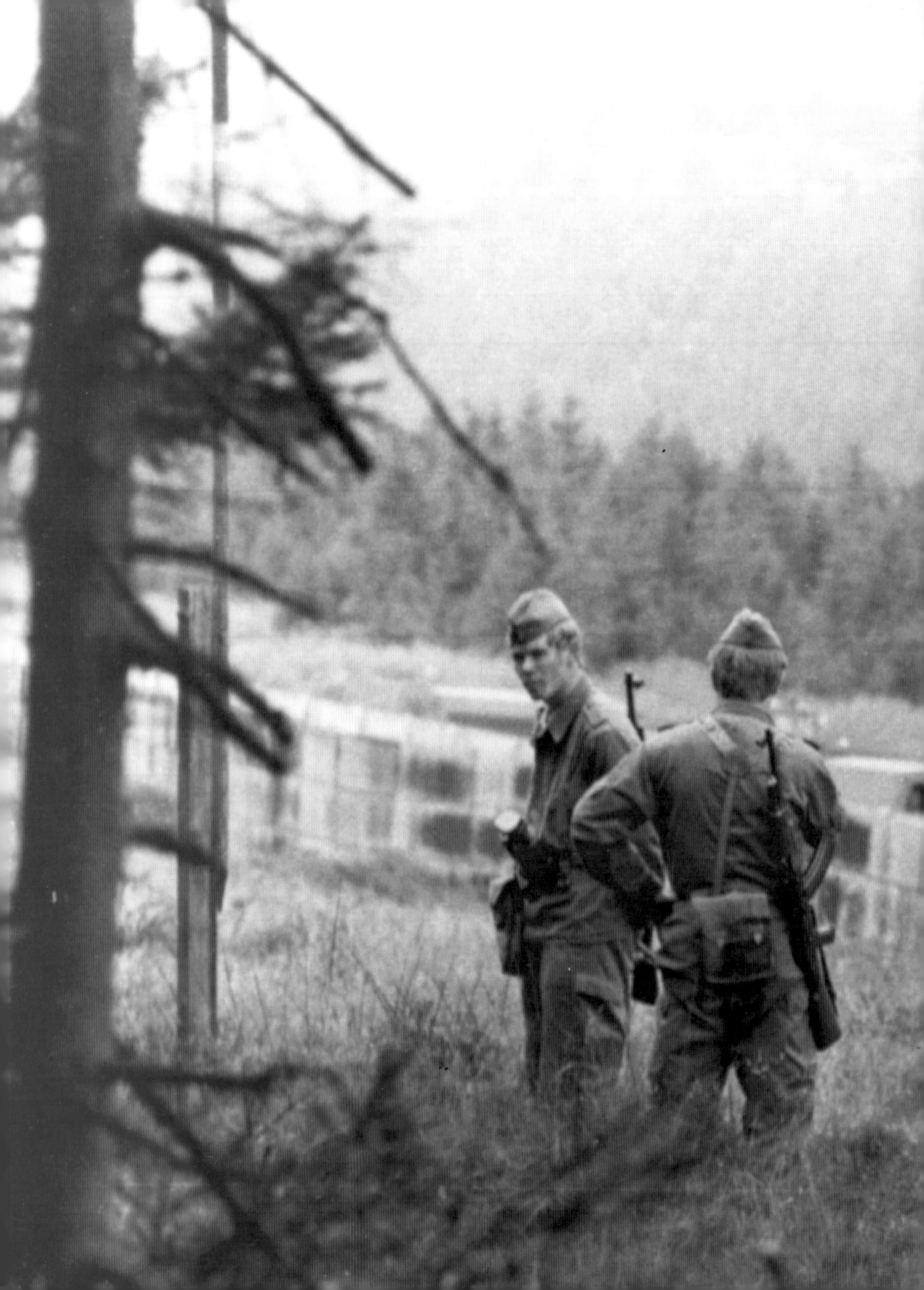

CHAPTER 2

Design and Development

If you take all the individual elements of the AK47 in isolation, at first it seems a rather unremarkable, even derivative weapon. Both the locking system and trigger group owe allegiance to the US M1 and M14 rifles.

The overall shape and configuration are strikingly similar to the German MP44. The gas-operation is conventional, with few distinguishing features. Yet it should be remembered that Kalashnikov was not designing a weapon to win design prizes, but to win battles. The nature of the design was secondary to the efficient application to its purpose, and Kalashnikov always acknowledged his borrowings from other people's firearms.

Yet what is true genius behind the AK47 is the unique combination of elements. Everything about the AK47 contributes to its reliability and solid combat performance. Thus there may be more ingenious weapons, but ingenuity rarely matters to the soldier in battle. What matters to him is that the gun works and continues to work, even through the dust, mud, debris and abuse of combat. This the AK47 does to an exemplary degree. This chapter will focus on how the AK47 functions, and why it has achieved its unparalleled popularity.

BASIC DESIGN AND OPERATION

Simply described, the AK47 is a gas-operated rotating-bolt assault rifle. Its gas-piston is sited above the barrel, it is fed from a curved 30-round box magazine, and its selector allows it to fire both single shots and full automatic. This description, however, does not do justice to Kalashnikov's intense labour that was recounted in Chapter 1. By describing how the AK47 works upon firing we can gain a more substantial insight into why the gun is such a convincing weapon to take into combat.

Firing the AK47 is simplicity itself. A fresh magazine is loaded, the charging handle is drawn back and released – thus stripping off the topmost cartridge of the magazine and

Left: East German soldiers on guard with their AK rifles. From 1948 the AK47 spread throughout Eastern Bloc forces before spilling over the communist borders to become a worldwide weapon.

pushing it securely into the chamber ready for firing. The selector switch is then pushed from the safety position to either the semi-automatic or full-automatic setting and the gun is then ready to fire (more about the actual process and technique of firing is covered in the next chapter).

The AK47 – like most modern weapons – fires from a closed-bolt position. (This means that the bolt is locked up against the breech prior to firing. Guns which fire from an open bolt have the disadvantage that the bolt system lurches forward on pulling the trigger and thus disrupts the firer's hold on the weapon and the overall accuracy of the shooting.) Being a rotating-bolt design, the AK47's bolt is locked into place for firing by two lugs which are rotated into seats machined into the receiver wall.

When the trigger is pulled, the trigger sear moves and releases the hammer. This drives forward onto the back of the firing pin which runs through the bolt. In turn, the firing pin strikes the primer of the cartridge and the round is fired. The bullet now begins its journey down the barrel, pushed by a wave of gas pressure from the propellant detonation and at a muzzle velocity of around 710mps (2329fps). At a point around 276mm (10.8in) from the back of the barrel – some two thirds of the barrel length – a small vent is situated at a backwards-facing 45° angle. Once the bullet has passed it, this vent diverts some of the firing gas upwards into the gas-cylinder situated just above the barrel. There it impinges on the face of a spring-loaded gas-piston, driving the piston backwards before the gas is vented out of the weapon. The backward force of the gas on the piston is the motive power which cycles the gun for the next shot. The piston is linked to the bolt carrier, thus as both are pushed backwards the bolt moves with them. To do this, however, the bolt lugs must first be rotated out of their seatings to unlock the bolt. This is accomplished by a cam on the carrier engaging with a lug on the bolt which disengages the bolt lugs once backward motion is applied.

Once the bolt is unlocked the entire bolt assembly moves back against the pressure of the recoil spring, riding over the hammer, while at the other end the spent cartridge is withdrawn and ejected smartly to the right of the gun as the breech fully opens. The force of the recoil spring eventually overcomes the backward motion of the bolt group and at this point it starts the bolt, bolt carrier and piston on their return journey. As the bolt is pushed forward it catches the top rim of the next cartridge, strips it from the magazine and then drives it forward into the breech. Here the bolt stops against the breech, but the carrier and piston continue for enough distance to enable the bolt-carrier cam and the bolt lug to perform rotational locking and thus secure the bolt for the firing of the next round.

Whether the next round is fired immediately or requires another pull of the trigger depends on whether full-auto-

Below: The top weapon here is the AKM rifle, while the bottom weapon is the Type 2 AK47 of forged steel construction, here broken down into its constituent parts during field stripping.

DESIGN AND DEVELOPMENT

matic or semi-automatic modes are selected respectively. If semi-automatic, then a disconnector in the trigger group prohibits the hammer being released forward until the trigger is pulled for a second time, and if automatic the disconnector is disengaged by the selector switch until pressure on the trigger is released.

This fairly detailed description of the operation of the AK47 does little to convey the reasons why the AK47 has attained the legendary status it has. What needs to be added to the equation is the element of simplicity. As will become clear, the AK47 is well-made from good materials, and each part of the weapon's function has little about it to go wrong as long as the weapon is reasonably well maintained. Even if it is not, the weapon will often function consistently well (though there will be more long-term wear upon its parts). The rotation of the bolt in locking is taken much further than many other assault rifles, and this solidity of action means that even the ingress of dirt will not usually prohibit the rifle functioning as it should. The simplicity of the AK47 is its primary virtue. Over time the inherent simplicity of the weapon was improved and sustained leading to the advent of its replacement, the AK74. But how did the AK47 evolve from the original prototype?

AK47: 1948–51

The first distinct period of the AK47's production and development reaches from just prior to its acceptance as a standard Soviet rifle in 1949 to 1951 when a significant change in production technique and design occurred. Initial pre-designation production of the AK47 had been located at the Tula arms factory, but by 1948 three plants were involved in the engineering of the new assault rifle. These were: Machine Engineering Plant #74 at Izhmash; the Mechanical Plant #622 at Izmekh; and the Izhevsk Motor Plant #524 in Izhevsk itself (the non-militaristic titles were used to elude Western intelligence). (To read a detailed history of the Izh arms plants refer to Val Shilin & Charles Cutshaw, *Legends and Reality of the AK:* Paladin Press, 2000.)

Production duties between these three sites were split. The first two plants listed generally made AK components which were then fed into the assembly units at Motor Plant #524. However, Izhmash soon started producing its own rifles and by early 1949 AK production was taken from Motor Plant #524 and given solely to Izhmash. Shilin & Cutshaw point out that this transfer took

Right: A private of the Egyptian Army stands at ease with his AKM rifle, bayonet fitted, in the Sinai desert in 1967. By the end of the 1960s Egypt would be manufacturing under licence its own AK type rifle, the Misr.

Above: A close-up of a stripped AK47. From top to bottom, the receiver cover, the return spring, the bolt mechanism and gas piston are all visible. Field stripping can be done in seconds by a trained user.

some time and both factories managed to produce 80,000 AKs between them in 1949.

The AKs of this early period – titled Type I by many for convenience – were defined by a production process that relied almost entirely on metal pressings and stampings for forming the receiver and many of its fittings. The advantages of stamping and pressing as opposed to machining parts from a solid block of steel are fairly extensive, and in the AK's case they can be read in the context of the Soviet Union's World War II industrial experience. As Edward Ezell has pointed out in his book *The AK47 Story* (Stackpole Books, 1986), the shortages in raw materials, skilled manpower and adequate machinery during World War II meant that many nations had to make weapons production as simple as possible without compromising the quality of the final firearm. Stamping and pressing from a sheet of steel could be done by semi-trained personnel (the real skill now lay in making the dies) and meant that wastage of metal was kept to an absolute minimum. Ezell gives the example of the German manufacture of the 20mm Flak 38 receiver housing. A machined receiver absorbed 45kg (99lb) of metal, whereas a stamped receiver took only 8.5kg (18.7lb). The stamping also took 70 per cent less time and 200 fewer items of machinery were required. Germany also pioneered the way in stampings and pressings applied to small arms in weapons such as the MP40 (the earlier MP38 had been machined) the MG42 and the STG44. Stamping became even more advantageous to Germany as the war went on and the major industrial centres came under regular destruction from Allied bombing. Stamped components could be made in smaller, less vulnerable engineering units with simple tools, so production could be dispersed rather than centred in big production plants visible to the bomb-aimer's eye. A more directly relevant example relates to the production of the Soviet PPSh41 and the PPS43. Both took increasing advantage of the new machine processes. Thus the PPSh41 took 7.3 hours each gun to make, while the PPS43 utilised stamping even more and each gun took only 2.7 hours to make. Steel consumption in the PPS43 was 6.2kg (13.6lb) as opposed to the PPSh41's 13.9kg (30.6lb).

The speed and economy of stamping, pressing and welding arms components was none the less relevant in the Soviet Union in the years immediately after the war, when post-war reconstruction and Cold War tensions required weapons to be produced quickly and cheaply. Kalashnikov's first AK was no exception. Between 1948 and 1951 the AK47 featured a stamped-steel receiver with riveted and welded plates. Only minor features of the receiver required machining – the insert for the barrel housing for example. The construction of the receiver helps define the first models from those which came later. The upper parts of the receiver visibly bend inwards, thus forming guides for the piston rod and bolt carrier group in firing. A date of production is usually stamped on the left side of the receiver along with a serial number and possibly a proof mark from the factory at which it was produced (two encircled crossed hammers indicate Tula; an arrow in a triangle indicates Izhevsk). The serial number is generally repeated just in front of the receiver on the right side and also on the back of the bolt covers. Early pressed selector switches consist of 'AB' over 'ОД' and are written in electric pencil in a somewhat rudimentary fashion.

The furniture of the AK47 in its early days used wood for the butt and fore-end, with the pistol grips being plastic but wood-laminated. The pistol-grip generally featured a chequered pattern to aid the firer's hold. Collapsible metal-stock varieties of AK were also produced, named the AKS. Like most folding-butt assault rifles, the AKS was designed for use by troops who operated in confined spaces, such as tank crew, vehicle drivers and airborne troops. This butt folded down and under the receiver. In this position the gun length was reduced to 700mm (27.5in) instead of the normal 870mm (34.25in). However, in the standard wooden-stock AK47 there was a trap in the butt which contained a basic cleaning kit, though the cleaning rod was situated beneath the barrel. The butt was fitted to the AK47 on two metal extensions which protruded from the rear of the receiver.

The magazines of the AK47 also had a design evolution. In the late 1940s these tended to be plain pressed steel without ribs. 30 M43 rounds were contained in these magazines, and the AK47's 775rpm rate-of-fire meant that these could be emptied in a matter of seconds when firing full automatic. Very optimistically, the top sights of the AK47 were graduated out to 800m (2624ft) – practical accuracy was more in the region of 300m (984ft). The business-end of the weapon was a 415mm (16.3in) barrel, chrome-lined for durability and having four right-hand grooves.

The Type I AK47 was a model of simple engineering and efficient construction. It was not only cheap to build but easy to fire. Yet Kalashnikov and his team were not complacent, and in 1951 they took a distinct step forward in the production of the weapon.

Below: Soviet women making PPSh41 submachine guns. New production methods using steel pressings slashed the manufacturing time and cost of firearms, hence the AK47's prodigious output.

THE AK47

Left: A Dhofari guerrilla of Oman in 1973, here seen with his AKM assault rifle. Due to its comprehensive distribution, AK weaponry become a dominant field weapon in most Middle Eastern conflicts.

AK47: 1951–59

In 1951, the production method of the AK47's receiver was switched from a stamping and pressing to more traditional machined processes. Considering our earlier notes about the advantages of pressed procedures, the step is unusual. Ezell suggests that the move was made because the post-war Soviet emphasis on manufacturing vehicles and aircraft took the requisite die-makers away to other sectors than small-arms manufacture. Thus the gun makers had to return to the more traditional lathes and drilling tools of machining. Shilin and Cutshaw argue that the production processes of stamping, pressing and welding weakened quality standards once the quotas of rifles increased. The arguments will continue for some time. AK47s from before 1951 often still work well today, though there is no denying that machined receivers are the stronger of the two formats.

Whatever the truth behind the debate, the 'Type II' went through its development life in the late 1940s and actually went into production from 1949 (thus the Soviet Ministry of Defence actually gave it the official designation 'AK49'). By 1951 the Type I was phased out in favour of this newer, more expensive weapon. As with the earlier examples of machined weapons, the Type II was incredibly wasteful to produce. It required a start line of 2.65kg (5.8lb) of steel which finished up in a receiver weighing no more than 0.65kg (1.43lb). Yet the Soviet authorities stuck with the machining process. The AK47 was additionally strengthened in the stock fixing. Out went the two metal extensions and in came a metal 'shoe' which slotted into the stock wood itself.

Identifying the Type II requires a subtle eye. All the furniture is of laminated wood, and the factory marks are exclusively of the Izhevsk type. The date and serial number can be found on the left side, sited in a milled depression in the receiver.

Though the Type II AK47 now had a rugged machined receiver and improved butt fixing, its evolution was far from over. Further research and development led to the Type III AK47. This was produced from 1954 until 1959. In many regards, the Type III was not that different from the Type II, except in the method of attaching the butt to the receiver. Instead of the metal shoe extension of the Type II, the Type III actually featured an insert extending from the butt itself which slotted into the end of the receiver and was securely bolted in place. This was the final act of design regarding the AK47 butt attachment, and the method of fitting became standard on the Type III and subsequent AK weapons.

The Type III became the most prolific of the classic AK47s. Machining processes were simplified to make the

DESIGN AND DEVELOPMENT

Left: The AK47 receiver. The large rectangular depression offset above the magazine housing disappeared with the AKM, which instead had a small lozenge-shaped recess square above the magazine.

gun easier to make in greater number, and the Type III also became the first of the AK weapons to be produced under licence in various Warsaw Pact and communist nations. By 1959 North Korea, Bulgaria, East Germany, Hungary, Poland and China were all producing there own AKs while Yugoslavia joined the group in 1964. The Type III weapons are not easy to define, but one of the best indicators of date is the manufacture of the magazine. From 1953 AKs received ribbed-steel magazines in contrast to the smooth metal surfaces of those prior to this date.

MODERNISING THE AK: THE AKM

In a sense, the Type III AK47 could be classed as the end of our story. The designation of AK47 would not be applied to any of the new breed of assault rifles after 1959. For in 1959 the Avtomat Kalashnikova Modernizirovannyi – Modernised Kalashnikov – or AKM, emerged and became the AK's dominant and most prolific form to this day.

The AKM is in every sense the fulfilment of the AK47. Experimentation surrounded the Kalashnikov weapons from the very first moment that Kalashnikov himself conceived of the weapon prototype. While the Type III signalled the end of the basic AK design, the technicians and weapons designers at Izhevsk were still engaged in vigorous experimentation to further improve this already superb weapon. Even during the early 1950s, a team of designers led by one Mikhail Miller experimented with shortened gas-systems and repositioned selector switches. They also toyed once more with sheet-metal stamping and pressing for the receiver construction.

The experiments steadily flushed out the good and the bad ideas. By the late 1950s the designers rolled out the new AKM, visually in keeping with the AK47 but with a radical overhaul of its manufacture and capabilities. It also signalled something of a return to old ways. Out went the machined receiver and the sheet-steel version returned, albeit a version much improved and strengthened by a U-shaped pressing.

Below: The fore-ends of the AK47 (bottom) and AKM (top) are here set in juxtaposition. The oblique-cut muzzle compensator on the AKM reduced the AK's tendency to climb up and right during full-auto fire.

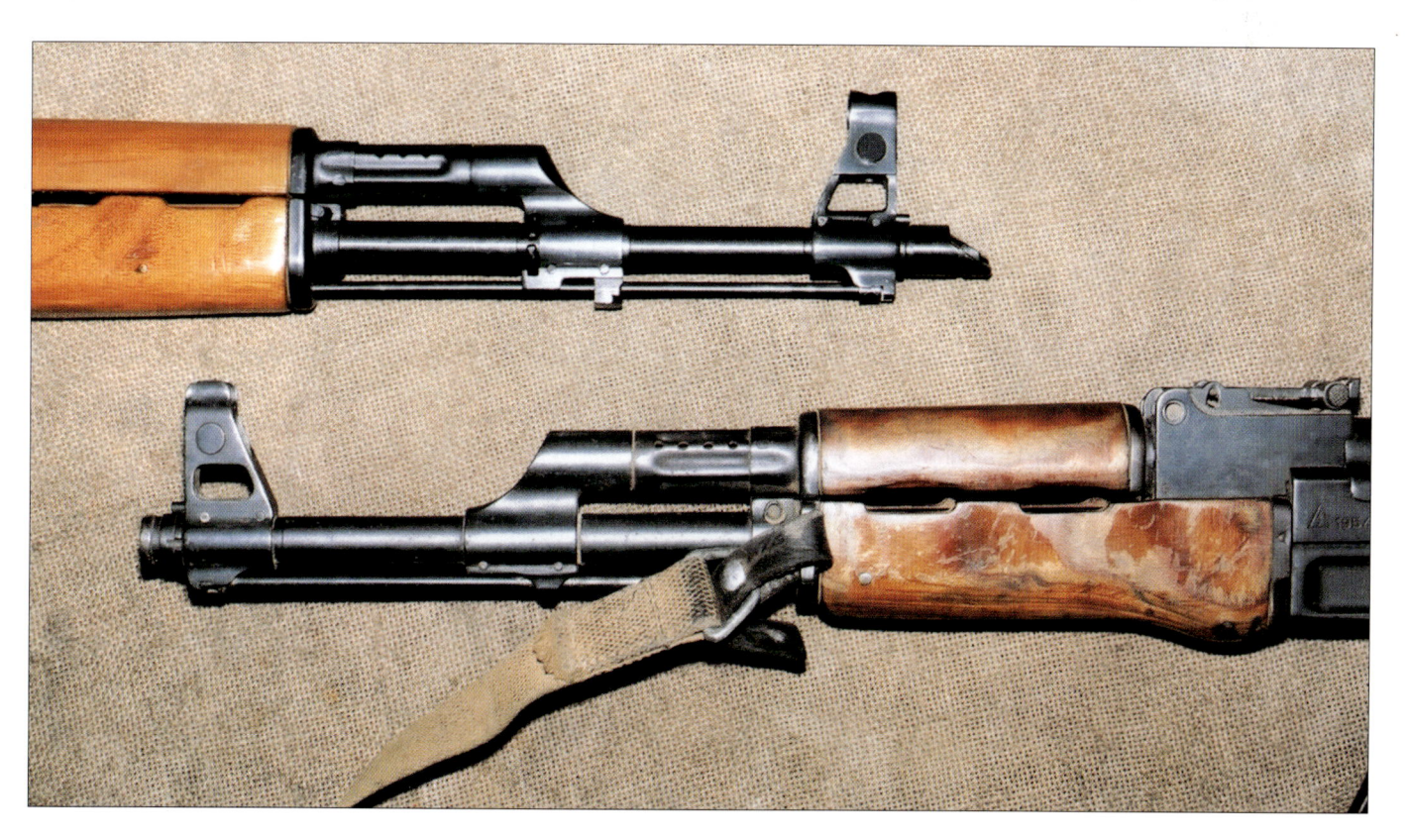

THE AK47

DESIGN AND DEVELOPMENT

Above: A unit of Romanian troops on patrol armed with AK47s and an RPD light machine gun. The AK47 became a standard Romanian assault rifle during the 1960s.

This return lightened the AK considerably. Whereas the AK47 weighed in at some 4.3kg (9.48lb), the AKM weighed 3.14kg (6.92lb). The surface of the receiver also differs from the AK47 by featuring two new rivets on each side just behind the fore-end stock, these being rivets holding in the bolt-lock recesses. There are also recesses stamped into the metal just above the magazine housing. These aided the secure and accurate seating of the magazine during loading by acting as guidance tracks.

The most significant change featured in the AKM was the fitting of a rate-reducing mechanism in the trigger group. The AKM trigger group is a totally new construction to that of the AK47. However, the central design change is the addition of a hammer-delay mechanism which imposes a minute resistance on the forward movement of the hammer when firing, just enough to take the cyclic rate of fire down to about 650rpm rather than 750rpm. The intention was to make the gun more controllable during automatic fire (it also made the gun less prone to firing through being jolted or banged), and this was assisted by an angular-cut muzzle compensator which deflected some muzzle blast upwards to deflect climb to the right. A further attempt at controlling the automatic-fire handling was made by switching the rotational action of

Left: A Serb soldier in Chechnya displays his AKM. In many of the former Soviet Union's regional conflicts, entire anti-government armies have been armed with black market or stolen AK weaponry.

the bolt locking from the right side to the left. As if misreading the implications of all these improvements, the designers recalibrated the rear sight to a distance of 1000m (3280ft) – exactly the sort of ranges which were considered infeasible during the development of the M43 round.

The receiver and trigger group were not the only foci of reworking. Composition and design of furniture also came in for attention. All furniture became wood laminated plastic – the plastic had more durable properties than the all-wood stocks commonly found on AK47s. The forestock was widened to aid grip and it featured two grip rails to give the hand greater purchase on the front end in wet or sweaty conditions. Even the folding metal stock was revised. Instead of being made from metal bar material the AKMS (the S suffix indicates folding stock) stocks were made from several pieces of stamped steel, and they are distinguished by a guttering which runs down the length of each strut. Also introduced to the AKM were plastic magazines. These magazines, made in a distinctive reddish-orange colour, did have metal magazine lips and magazine base plate, but the ribbed metal variety continued in widespread use.

The AKM, like the AK47, could play host to many different types of accessory. Silencers such as the PBS-1 could be

29

THE AK47

Above: Russian soldiers in arctic conditions prepare to fire their AK rifles and an RPK squad automatic weapon. Even in such sub zero environments, the AK would offer excellent reliability.

fitted, screwed onto the muzzle once the compensator had been removed. Standard optical, NSP-2 infra-red or NSPU image-intensifier sights could all be fitted, as could GP-26 grenade launchers. The bayonet, however, deserves a special mention. AK47s had almost all featured bayonet lugs, but the AKM took a new style of bayonet that served purposes other than combat. The AKM bayonet was designed by Todorov, a Soviet Naval officer. The bayonet had a hole cut right through which engaged with a lug on the scabbard and turned the knife into a two section wire-cutting device. (Todorov origi-

MODES OF WEAPON OPERATION

Firearms have many methods of operation, but during the twentieth century self-loading weapons generally fell into one of four operating systems:

Blow-back
When a blow-back weapon is fired, the bolt is not locked but simply holds the cartridge in place through the inertia of the return spring. The pressure of firing builds until the force of the return spring is overcome and slams the bolt backwards. On its backward journey the spent cartridge is extracted and ejected before the force of the return spring begins the cycle again. Blow-back tends to be confined to submachine gun and handgun operation, as anything more than a pistol-calibre round would require a massive and heavy bolt and would create handling problems through recoil force.

Recoil
A recoil-operated gun is cycled by the force of the barrel recoiling upon firing. The barrel is locked together with the bolt and both recoil backwards until the chamber pressure reaches safe levels. At this point the bolt unlocks from the barrel and continues backwards on its own, completing ejection before moving back again stripping the next round from the magazine and closing up with the barrel again for firing. Recoil operation is separated into two types: short recoil, when the barrel and bolt recoil for less than the length of the cartridge before unlocking, and long recoil when the two components actually travel together for a greater distance than the full cartridge length.

Gas-operation
This is the most common method of operation for assault rifles and many machine guns. In this case the gun is cycled by gas being bled off from the barrel and used against the piston or the bolt to drive the bolt backwards and cycle the gun in preparation for the next round. The AK47 utilises this method. Gas-operation generally has the virtue of reliability.

DESIGN AND DEVELOPMENT

nally designed the knife for Spetsnaz special forces, a common part of their naval operation being cutting through enemy barbed wire defences on shore positions.) Both the knife and the scabbard were also insulated to protect the user against possible shock from electrified wire. As a bayonet the AKM knife has limited application, but otherwise it is a capable fighting knife which has a substantial practicality. Its design has influenced many others, such as the British Army, to provide a knife for their troops with similar properties and the German Army also used the AKM bayonet as standard issue on their G36 rifles.

Visually, all the changes in the AKM make it a fairly easy gun to distinguish (further defining traits include an absence of gas vents in the piston wall). The AKM was the last in the AK47 series proper – that is the Kalashnikov rifle designed around the 7.62mm M43 cartridge. In the early 1970s the changes in world-wide rifle production towards small-calibre high-velocity cartridges saw the Kalashnikov recalibrated for the 5.45mm round and designated the AK74. More about this weapon and other AK variants is contained in Chapter 5. Yet the AK47 design continues to this day around the world, and derivative or licensed production adds to the 80 million AK type weapons already made.

Furthermore, recent AK74 weapons have also made a return to the 7.62 x 39mm M43 cartridge in the form of guns such as the AK103 and AK104. These weapons are essentially the same as the AK74, but recalibrated for the M43; in the case of the AK104 it has a shorter barrel for use as a submachine gun.

Such was the success of the AK47's operating system, that it also went on to feature in whole different classes of weapons (again covered in more detail in Chapter 5). Machine guns such as the RPK, sniper rifles like the SVD Dragunov, even shotguns such as the Sayga, have kept the AK standard alive in multiple formats. Add the variations developed outside of the Soviet Union and CIS and your are left with a bewildering variety of AK derivatives which still pay homage to the original design laid down by Kalashnikov over 50 years ago. The next chapter will examine, in as much detail as space will allow, the practicalities of actually handling the AK47, and the skilled training involved in its expert use.

Below: Polish troops prepare to split the woodland silence with bursts from their PMK assault rifles. Braced on the trees, these weapons should be able to command good accuracy up to 300m (984ft).

THE AK47

AKS47

Left: A Romanian soldier stands guard bearing an AKM. His weapon is fitted with a foregrip and he presents a clear view of the AK bayonet's wire-cutting mechanism.

AMMUNITION

Before moving on to this, however, it is worth classifying some of the standard types of M43 ammunition fired by the AK rifles. The ballistic properties and combat effectiveness of the M43 is explored in more detail in Chapter 4. Here the classifications of ammunition will be discussed as well as how each type is identified.

Sticking strictly with Soviet type ammunition, there are around four specific types of M43 ammunition. Regardless of the type, however, they are all 7.62 x 38.6mm, rimless, in a coppered steel case. The standard round, known as the PS, is boat-tailed (i.e. it narrows at the base, thus reducing flight drag when the round drops to subsonic speed) with a cartridge base diameter of just under 11mm (0.43in) and has a lead jacket over a tombak-coated steel sheath which contains a stamped steel core. This combination allows good adhesion to the rifling when passing down the barrel while the inner core stops deformation of the bullet on impact. It is held firmly into the cartridge case by having a cannelure running around it into which the case edge engages after crimping. Weight is 7.9gm (0.28oz).

DESIGN AND DEVELOPMENT

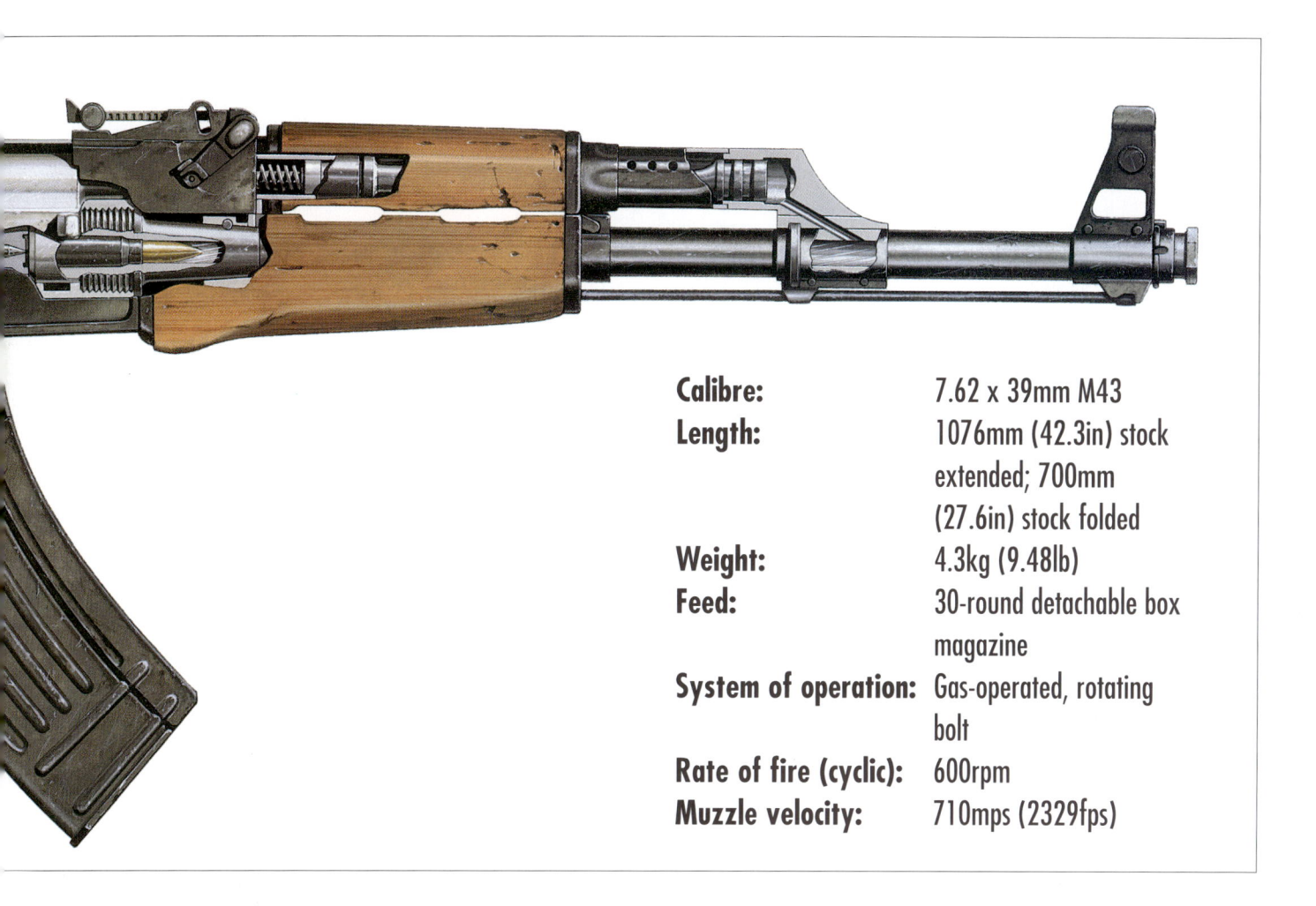

Calibre:	7.62 x 39mm M43
Length:	1076mm (42.3in) stock extended; 700mm (27.6in) stock folded
Weight:	4.3kg (9.48lb)
Feed:	30-round detachable box magazine
System of operation:	Gas-operated, rotating bolt
Rate of fire (cyclic):	600rpm
Muzzle velocity:	710mps (2329fps)

Next in the sequence is the 'Z' incendiary. This contains incendiary materials that both illuminate the round in flight as a red dot and which also ignite the target materials on impact. Combustion is achieved by a tombak-coated steel cup in the nose of the bullet which is filled with an incendiary pellet and ruptured by the steel core on impact. When the target is struck the core hits a priming mixture at the bottom of the cup which ignites the pellet; the product of this combustion spills out as the cup itself is ruptured by the core. Weighing 6.6gm (0.23oz), the Z has a flat instead of a boat-tailed base and is marked with a red tip.

One step on from the T-45 is the BZ. This is an armour-piercing incendiary round for use against lightly armoured vehicles and fuel tanks. In many ways the BZ is constructed like the Z round but its steel core is hardened to perform its armour-piercing function (the Z is only effective against up to 3mm/0.1in of steel plate). The BZ weighs 7.8gm (0.27oz) and features a black tip above a red band. The final bullet in the range is the T-45 tracer bullet. In this round the tombak-coated steel cup contains a trace compound and an incendiary material, the latter lit by firing gases in the barrel and this in turn lighting the trace compound for the flight. Unlike the PS it has a flat base and is designated by a green tip.

The properties of the 5.45mm bullet used in the AK74 are analysed in Chapter 4 and Chapter 5. The subject of ammunition reminds us of the issue that whatever the design skill behind the AK47 and its successors, its purpose is to kill. How soldiers are trained to use it for this task is the subject of the following chapter.

AWARDS AND RECOGNITION

As the father of the AK47 Mikhail Timofeyevich Kalashnikov made one of the most seminal contributions to weapons design of any engineer in Soviet, indeed global, history. Recognition for his work has come not only from the acknowledgement of his peers and historians, but also from the Soviet authorities. The Socialist awards he has received include two Hero of Socialist Labour, three Orders of Lenin, one Order of the October Revolution, an Order of the Red Star (given for wartime service as a tank commander), an Order of the People's Friendship, and an Order of the Labour Red Banner. He also has received Lenin and State Prize Laureates. The range of his awards hints at some of the political power that has accrued to Kalashnikov. He has performed several periods of service as a member of the Supreme Soviet, and stands as a popular figure in Soviet history.

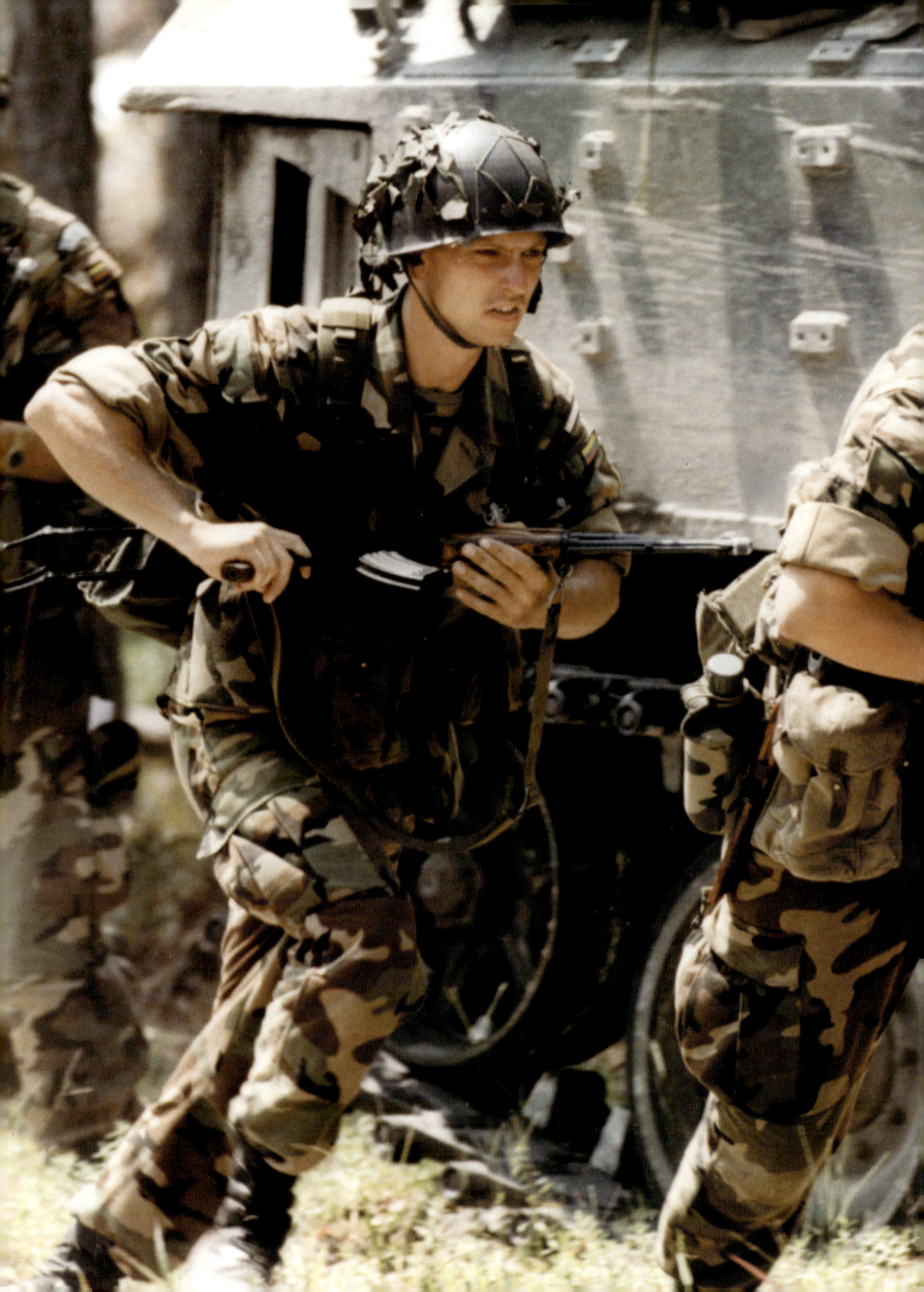

CHAPTER 3

Usage and Training

It is impossible to generalise about using the AK47. With some 80 million (including foreign variants) distributed around the world, its tactical applications have ranged from a random burst from an open window by an untrained terrorist, to major fire coordination from massed troops of a regular army.

The diverse application of the AK47 is such that it cannot be the subject of sweeping statements. However, it is possible to assess the fundamentals of its usage and the basic training required if the weapon is to be used at its most effective. This chapter will examine the essential combat use of the AK47 – how to load it, fire it, and what sort of tactical considerations are required. First, it is worth looking at how the AK47 changed the forces for which it was originally designed.

SOVIET AND WARSAW PACT TACTICS

AK firepower transformed the potential of Soviet and Warsaw Pact forces from the moment of its introduction. In Cold War studies, this transformation is rarely charted, mainly because it is difficult to assess the impact of small arms on a major tactical scale. Missile systems, tanks, combat shipping and aircraft have all hogged the limelight, and understandably so. Small arms are controlled not by large-scale strategic policies, but by individual combat skill which is less open to evaluation. What can be said, however, is that the introduction of the AK47 to Soviet units radically altered their close–medium range offensive and defensive possibilities.

Apart from the period under Kruschev's premiership, when nuclear arsenals were developed at the expense of regular units, the post-war Soviet regime made intense efforts to keep its soldiery up to speed with Western strengths and tactics. Most military authorities at the time envisaged a major East-West clash as taking place across Russia's flat borderlands, and consequently the Soviet Union geared its troops

Left: Romanian troops sprint into action from an APV during exercises. The compressed dimensions of the AK rifles make them ideal for deployment in the hands of armoured troops.

THE AK47

towards major land offensives which harked back to World War II battles such as Kursk.

Soviet ground divisions were classified according to three main types – Motor-Rifle, Tank and Airborne. The bulk of the ground forces (numbering about two million in the early 1970s) was composed of Motor-Rifle Divisions, each division comprising some 13,000 front line troops divided into operational battalions of around 450 men. Elite airborne troops numbered only about eight divisions at peak strength.

The implications for the Soviet forces of the introduction of the AK47 changed the possibilities of infantry tactics. Because of the rapid advance in military technology following World War II, the ability to deliver heavy accurate firepower at a focused point of aggression became paramount. Overall strategies amongst Soviet high command remained fairly conventional – encirclement and pinpoint blitzkrieg-style attacks were the most common offensive perceptions.

Yet at a close tactical level Soviet military thinkers recognised that what was decisive was both the aggression contained in the attack, plus the superiority in men (numbers and training) and matériel at the point of clash. Because the Cold War Soviet Union would not be able to access the levels of conscription utilised in World War II (World War III was predicted as a very quick conflict decided by superior technology), the emphasis on superior weaponry was essential to raising expectations of victory.

Here the AK47 makes an entry. During World War II, the majority of soldiers had long-range Mosin-Nagant M1891 rifles with the fortunate remainder having close-range submachine guns such as the PPSh41 and PPS43. The disparity between these two styles of weapons meant that achieving a constant tempo or meaningful strategy of personal firepower was difficult, and more often than not the heavy machine gunners were relied on to sway the battle. With the standardisation of the AK47, however, all that changed. For the first time Soviet troops could rely on being able to generate consistent levels of firepower at the 0–300m (0–984ft) range which was accurate, powerful, reliable and dense. Each Soviet or Warsaw Pact foot soldier could run through a magazine of 30 7.62mm rounds in a matter of seconds. Multiply this by the 450 men of a regular-sized battalion and it was envisaged that at least in personal combat the Soviet forces could outshoot their opponents.

Why this would be important is more clearly seen by a look at a central pillar of Soviet tactical thought – the 'Encounter Battle'. The encounter battle was based on a scenario in which an attacking Soviet column meets an advancing enemy column head on. Soviet thinking judged that against Western forces this would be a situation in which the

Left: A private of the Soviet Army stands guard in Budapest in 1956. Though Soviet armour did not perform well in the Hungarian uprising, the AK47 showed itself to be an excellent firearm for urban combat.

USAGE AND TRAINING

Red Army would have the advantage, mainly because British and US armoured vehicles were thought to be less manoeuvrable than Soviet equivalents in mobile warfare. A textbook encounter battle would run thus. The Soviet and enemy forces clash head on, but Soviet forces quickly strip off a flanking column under guidance of reconnaissance groups. This, following a short artillery bombardment, punctures the enemy column from the flank. With great violence, this flanking attack would actually punch deep into the enemy troops to fight at close quarters, a form of combat in which the Soviets had a great deal of confidence following World War II engagements such as Stalingrad.

The very emphasis is on close-quarter battle which is the territory of the AK47. Each armoured fighting vehicle would usually have five AK47s or AKMs on board, and each foot soldier would be able to deliver short, hacking bursts of fire into the compact enemy columns. Other Kalashnikov weapons, such as the RPK machine gun, would be able to provide cover fire at ranges of up to 800m (2624ft). The storm of firepower that massed AK47s would be able to produce would be very convincing in combat at visual ranges (see Chapter 4). While in the early days of the Cold War enemy troops might be firing M14s (prior to the introduction of the M16) or FN FALs – both guns which were awkward in putting down automatic fire because of the full-power cartridges they used – the Soviet troops would have a weapon that could fire full automatic yet retain a controllable accuracy.

One of the greatest advantages of the AK47 apart from this battlefield capability was its ease of use. The AK47 had manageable recoil. Its operating principles were exceptionally straightforward. It would rarely fail in action. As such the Kalashnikov weapons had the ideal ratio of quick training to credible combat results. But what are the fundamentals of operating and maintaining this weapon? By examining this we will understand more of what made the AK weapons so legendary.

FIRING THE AK47

Few assault rifles can be simpler than the AK47 to fire. From its first origins, the AK47 was designed to be a fighter's gun.

Below: Here an AK74 rifle has been adapted as a port firing weapon on a BMP-2 tank. The 5.45mm calibre can be identified by the grooves in the butt and the shallower curve of the magazine.

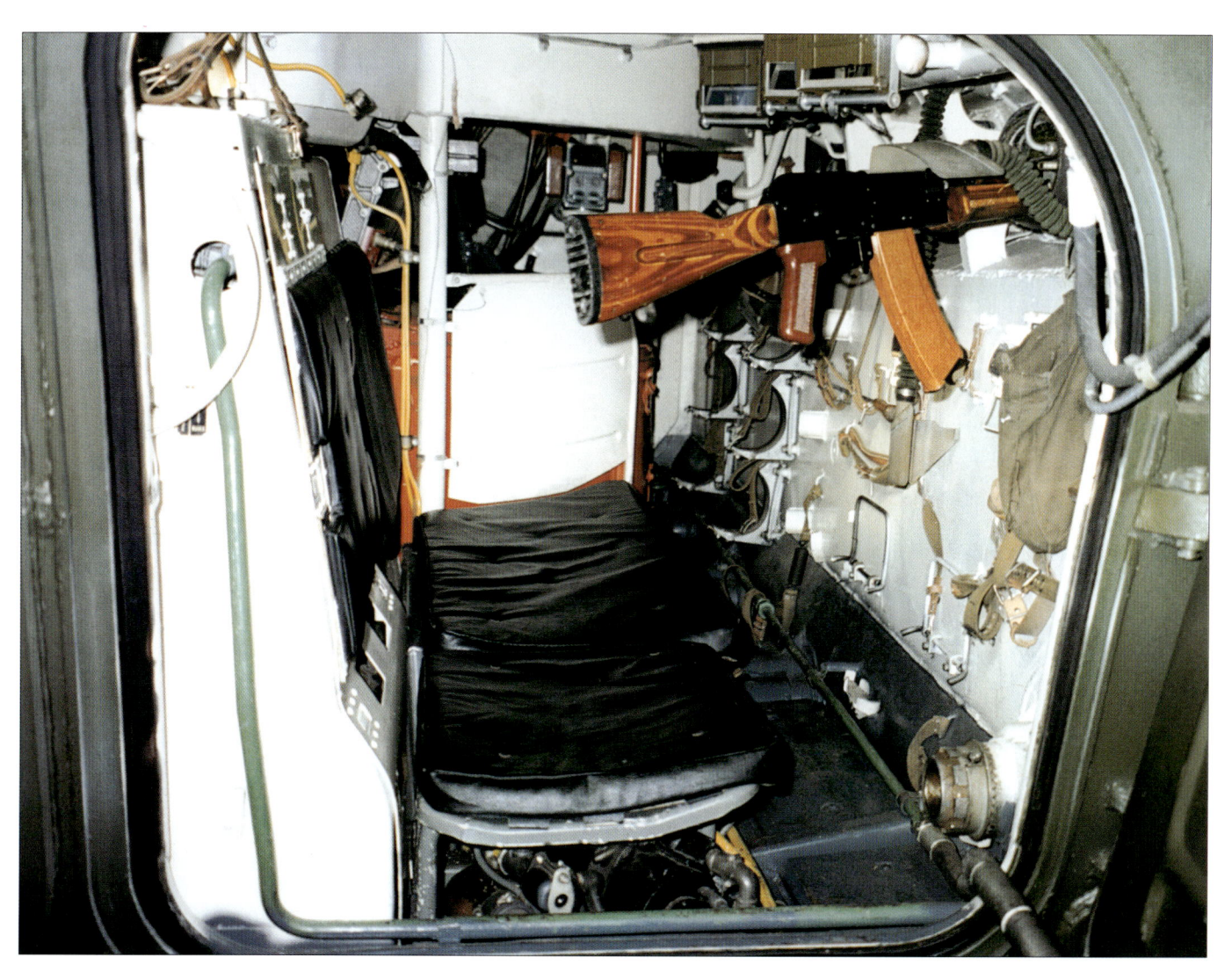

Above: Soviet troops leap from a T54 tank during a training exercise. These troops comprise a typical Red Army squad; most are armed with AK rifles while support fire is provided by an RPK-armed soldier.

It did away with sophistication in form and replaced it with solidity in function. The firing process begins, as with most assault rifles, with the loading of the magazine. In the vast majority of cases AK rifles are used with 30-round curved magazines constructed of either pressed steel or plastic (the latter having metal magazine lips and base plate for more reliable feed). There are exceptions to this size, particularly in relation to Chinese-type AKs. Chinese weapons can also be seen with 5-, 20-, and 40-round magazines and, more unusually, with 40- and 75-round drums (even a 99-round drum is available). The experiments with high-capacity magazines have rarely taken hold. During the 1950s, the Soviet Union also constructed an experimental magazine for the AK which maintained its curve right up to the muzzle and which contained some 100 rounds. This magazine, like the high-capacity Chinese drum magazines, were easily damaged however, and the pursuit of such feeds ceased in the USSR.

All soldiers in formal armies are trained to treat their AK magazines with as much care as the gun itself. AK magazines are of a solid construction, but if they become dirty or the lips become damaged then feed will be unpredictable and problematic. Thus when not in use the magazines should be stored away in their custom-made kit pouches. With Soviet kit these pouches were generally issued in olive-green and had one pouch for every two magazines, two of these hanging from the soldier's belt. Other forms of carriage were applied in different countries. Returning to the Far East, Chinese, North Korean, North Vietnamese and Viet Cong soldiers used the 'Chi Com' (standing for Chinese Communist) pattern of battle order dress, the magazines being hung across the chest in curved pouches.

Loading the magazines is simply a matter of inserting single rounds down through the lips against the feed spring. Optionally, ten rounds can be loaded at once via SKS rifle chargers used with an AK47 magazine adapter. One common trick used by Soviet soldiers and troops to this day was to place two or three tracers at the bottom of the magazine. During firing and combat these would indicate that the magazine was running low, something made more important by the fact that AKs do not have a bolt hold-open device to inspect the level of ammunition feed. Most soldiers will also refrain from filling the magazine repeatedly up to its full capacity, as this can weaken the spring over time and lead to further feed problems.

USAGE AND TRAINING

Right: A private of the Cuban Army here seen in Angola in 1976. His AKM rifle is supplemented by the practical AKM bayonet, the wire-cutting mechanism clearly seen at the tip of the scabbard.

Once the magazine is loaded, it is tapped against a hard surface a couple of times to make sure that all the cartridges are seated properly, and then it is inserted into the gun. AK47 magazines are sited by first inserting the leading edge into the magazine housing, then swinging the rest of the magazine up into the housing with a brisk hinging motion (on an AKM the two indentations just above the magazine housing act as further guides to proper seating). Once the magazine is properly in place, the cocking handle on the top right-hand side is pulled back and released, usually by reaching over with the left arm (for right-armed shooters). Once released the cocking handle strips the first round from the magazine, inserts it into the chamber, and the gun is loaded.

To fire the gun, the thumb of the trigger hand depresses the large pressed-metal selector switch from its uppermost 'Safe' position to either its first selection, semi-automatic, or the full automatic selection beneath it. The selector switch itself has been something of a cause for concern for all combat users of AK rifles. Its fairly crude construction produces a loud 'clack' noise when being operated, a noise with enough volume to blow the cover on an ambush or other operation. Combat soldiers discovered that this problem could be mostly alleviated by bending the selector switch slightly up and away from the receiver and wrapping tape around it to prevent metal banging against metal when the switch was used.

Once the mode of fire is selected the gun will fire at the pull of the trigger. Most soldiers have found that the trigger pull on the AK47 is not especially satisfying. It tends to have a long period of draw before suddenly snapping off a round. This can compromise accurate aiming, but practically the gun can still be used with confidence at the usual combat ranges of around 150m (492ft).

Sighting is provided as standard by basic iron sights. The back sight is a simple V notch configuration. On the AK47 this is graduated up to 800m (2624ft); on the AKM 1000m (3280ft). Both ranges are wildly beyond what the AK guns are capable of, so soldiers tend to set the sights mostly at a maximum of about 300m (984ft) range. The V notch is aligned to a simple frontal pin. The pin is framed by either two 'ears' or by a ring, and on later versions of the AKs it featured a luminous Tritium dot which acts as an aid to shooting in low-light conditions. (Additionally, luminous inserts can be added to standard iron sights, both front and back, through adapter kits.) Some training is required to master the iron sights for combat use. The US M16 assault rifle has a rear tubular peep sight, an intermediary V and a final pin. The three stages of this sighting arrangement make the rifle very easy to align on a shifting target – as long as the target is seen through the peep sight then the other sights will quickly

39

THE AK47

USAGE AND TRAINING

seem to align with it. By contrast, the AK47 requires slightly more of a 'shotgun style' of aiming in a rapid-reaction situation. The initial lead is gained from the front of the gun rather than the rear and it takes some hours of training to be able quickly to square the back V up with the pin. Despite this, and also despite the fact that the rear sight is prone to knocks, the AK47 has never seemed to have problems putting down accurate fire in combat situations, and modern 5.45mm rifles like the AK74 are as capable as their western equivalents.

Apart from iron sights, a variety of optical sights are also available for the AK rifles. Originally the fitting of these had to be somewhat improvised as mounting rails were not always provided. The soldier had to exercise particular care that the sight did not interfere with either the loading or the operation of the weapon. In the last 20 years most AKs have emerged from factories with sight rails cut in place to overcome this problem. Because the practical range of the AK is so limited, most of the optical sights used are not intended

Left: A Polish army reconnaissance group stops for observations during armoured manoeuvres. While the officer makes an assessment he is framed by two AK-armed soldiers prepared to deliver support fire.

Above: A squad of Soviet rocket men in firearms training. Note the loading action: the front edge is inserted into the housing first, then the magazine is hinged backwards to lock into place.

for long-range sniping use. Generally AK optical sights are either thermal imaging or image intensifying by nature, giving the AK user a capacity to operate in low-light or nighttime conditions. Originally such sights could be enormously bulky. Some almost stretched the length of the entire weapon and stood many inches above the receiver. Soldiers using such an arrangement had to train themselves to move cautiously through undergrowth and in urban environments to stop the sight catching on objects and being knocked out of alignment. Yet in recent years a new generation of slimmer sights has emerged, especially as thawing relations with the West have provided access to the latest in US and German sighting technology.

The principles of firing the AK47 for best effect are common to most assault rifle training. An important choice in combat is the selection of either full- or semi-automatic fire. The general principle for most using the rifle is to stick with semi-automatic unless there is the need to 1) provide heavy suppressing fire; 2) utilise firepower in close-quarters; or 3) maximise impact on massed troops at long ranges. Even these three sets of conditions can be handled using semi-automatic fire. The problem for the AK user is that the full-automatic rate of fire is so high that magazines take only three or four seconds to empty and overall ammunition is depleted quickly. Additionally, automatic fire encourages slipshod aiming, and it is far more effective to choose a defined target and put out deliberately aimed rounds than to spray hopefully in the general direction. A halfway house that the Kalashnikov family has avoided is the useful three-round burst, and the AN94 rifle which hints at being the AK74's replacement has this function. However, three-round burst facilities add to the complexity of a weapon and make it more vulnerable to failure. By contrast, the AK would rarely fail and as long as the soldier practised on the firing range his hit rate would be good. Regular use would also give the soldier the trigger dexterity to fire off two or three rounds at a time.

Below: Soviet troops during an exercise on one of the Soviet Union's southern frontier posts. Typically, several members of the squad would advance under AK covering fire before switching roles to allow the others to advance.

Before passing on to the subject of maintenance, it is worth reflecting on how the adoption of the 5.45 x 39 M74 cartridge has changed the experience of firing the AK rifle. The AK74 (covered in greater depth in Chapter 5) is part of the new small-calibre high-velocity family of weapons which emerged into the arms trade in the late 1960s and 1970s. Those familiar with the AK47 will find little truly unfamiliar when they pick up an AK74, though they will instantly feel the weight difference between the AK47's 4.3kg (9.4lb) and the AK74's 3.6kg (7.9lb) empty weight. They will, however, feel quite different sensations upon firing, sensations which also make the weapon even more conducive to fire-control training than the AK47.

The 5.45mm round makes very little recoil when fired. Soviet scientific analysis showed that whereas the AKM rifle packed 7.19 joules of recoil force, the AK74 slashed that figure down to 3.39 joules (this is almost half the recoil force of the M16A1, another small-calibre weapon). Furthermore, the high velocity of the AK74 round (900mps/2952fps) gives the AK74 2.5 times the genuine effective range of its predecessor. Much of the reason for the low recoil lies in an effective muzzle brake and compensator unit which diverts the

USAGE AND TRAINING

Right: Four AK magazines. From smallest to largest they are a 20-round magazine, the standard 30-round, a 40-round, and a home-made 55-round magazine, the latter made by joining a 30- and 40-round magazine together.

muzzle gases out to the side and also controls muzzle climb. Thus the AK74 user has much more control over the rifle during those periods of automatic fire, and finds the AK74s three-round-burst facility consequently much more useful.

The AK74 is also much quieter than the AK47, but the AKM can be fitted with various types of silencers. Fitting silencers such as PBS-1 necessitates the removal of the muzzle brake/compensator. Once removed the silencer screws onto the end of the muzzle. A PBS-1 is a ten-baffle silencer which reduces the AK47 percussion to a sound akin to a .22in rifle being fired. The user must treat his silenced weapon in a very different manner to his normally configured firearm. If normal rounds are used with a silencer, then the silencer unit will wear out extremely quickly and the

Below: East German soldiers during a weapon cleaning session. Though the AK does not need much cleaning, regular maintenance will dramatically improve its longevity.

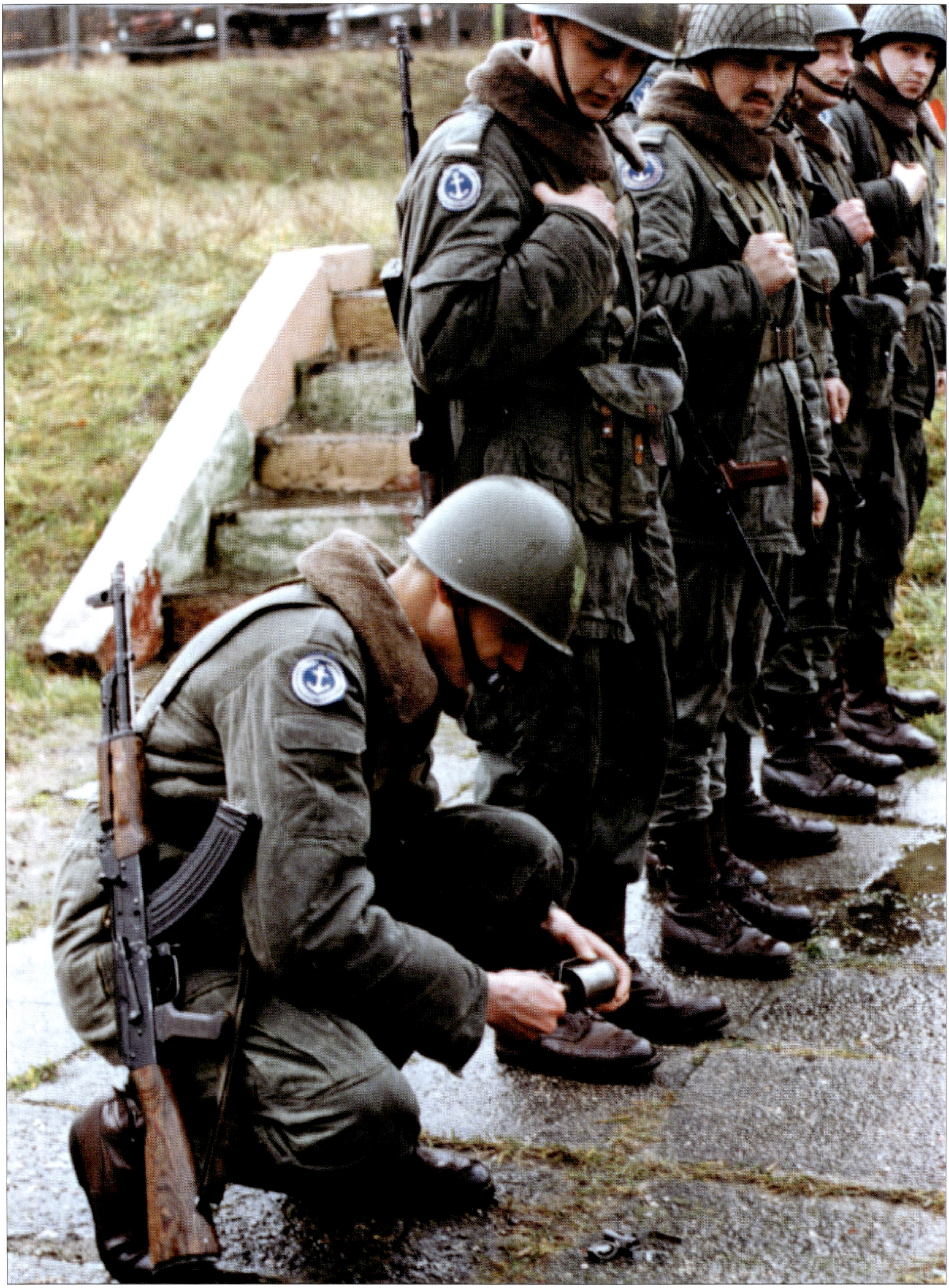

USAGE AND TRAINING

Left: Polish infantry during weapons instruction wear their AKMs slung over their shoulders. The ammunition pouches at the front of their uniforms would typically contain four spare magazines.

silenced effect will be undone by the loud crack of supersonic bullets. Thus silenced AKs tend to use reduced-power charges which keep the bullet below the speed of sound but also dramatically curtail the effective range of the weapon. Hence regular army units rarely train with silenced AKs, and they remain the province of special forces units who are skilled in behind-the-lines operations.

Whether handling an AK47 or an AK74, silenced or not, Kalashnikovs are not difficult guns to fire, but practice is required to do it well. The same has to be said for the principles of maintaining the AK47.

MAINTENANCE

Like any piece of weapons engineering, the AK47 needs regular maintenance if it is to perform with the reliability for which it is famous. This essentially means becoming dextrous in the procedures of field stripping. Field stripping is the process of cleaning the gun's vital mechanisms. Training in professional armies, the former Soviet Union included, always devotes significant slabs of time to field stripping. It is a routine which must become second nature to a soldier, and something which he can perform without even looking at the weapon in case of the need for field stripping in night-time conditions.

The intention of field stripping is to clean the barrel, bolt and gas system from any invasive materials such as dirt, pieces of material, and from build-ups of corrosive chemicals from the process of firing. Because AKs are so globally present, the ammunition which is fed in to them is not always of the best quality. Communist ammunition in particular is naturally widespread, and its generally lower standards of production result in corrosive residues in the barrel and gas assembly after periods of firing. Thankfully, cleaning an AK47 is a straightforward procedure which requires no special tools. All the tools needed are contained within the rifle itself. The wooden stock features a brass-lidded trap which contains a basic cleaning kit – brushes, oil, and one or two wrenches. A cleaning rod hangs underneath the barrel.

The field-stripping procedure on the AK47 follows straightforward lines:

1. Firstly, the magazine is removed by pressing forward the magazine release catch situated just in front of the trigger guard. The magazine should come out easily. For safety, at this point the bolt should be drawn back and released to check that there is not still a round in the chamber. After this the trigger should be pulled (with the gun pointing at the ground) as an extra precaution.

2. With the magazine clear, use the thumb to push in the retaining lever button which is situated on the flat back end of the receiver cover. Pushing this in disconnects the top of the receiver – lift the receiver cover up and back and it will come free from the gun.

3. The return spring and retaining rod will now be exposed. Take hold of them and firmly push them forward, then lift them up and back to remove them from the gun.

4. Now you are able to remove the bolt and bolt carrier. This is done by drawing back the cocking handle; both elements should come free. Once removed, it is then possible to separate the bolt and the bolt carrier. This is done by twisting the bolt counter-clockwise and then drawing it out of the carrier.

5. The field strip is completed by opening up and cleaning the gas system. The gas system is opened by undoing the gas-cylinder lock on the right of the rear sight block. This then allows the gas piston to be withdrawn and lifted out and the bore of the cylinder is exposed.

As the field stripping process is undertaken, each part should be cleaned with the right brushes and lightly oiled where appropriate. Oil should never be too thick or delivered to excess, as heavy oil deposits attract grit and dust and the mixture is especially abrasive to the fine tolerances of moving gun parts. The barrel should almost never be oiled and the gas piston rarely oiled – both of these parts can suffer from scaling or abrasions once the weapon is heated up under firing.

Field stripping is a diligent practice, and the military user should be particularly careful that all parts are free from the lint of cleaning pads after field maintenance has taken place. On some occasions complete disassembly of the weapon might be necessitated. This is not the province of the soldier but of the experienced gunsmith or armourer. Yet it is rarely necessary to go to such lengths. The AK47 and its derivatives will give few problems if basic field stripping is followed regularly.

So what can be said in fact about the AK's legendary reliability? Certainly in the early firing tests of the AK prototypes, astounding results were achieved. Some World War II Russian submachine guns were calculated to jam at the frightening rate of every 20 rounds. By contrast, if fed with good quality ammunition and kept in solid working order the AK47 would reduce that rate to more like 30,000 rounds before a jam. Testing of the early Kalashnikovs saw them mistreated in a variety of ways – plunged into water, buried in sand and mud, repeatedly banged against hard surfaces – and almost always the AK came out of each test firing normally.

When problems do occur, however, there are several predominant causes that the operator should look out for.

WEAPONS OF A SOVIET INFANTRYMAN

In addition to an AK assault rifle, Soviet infantrymen carried a range of other personal weapons. Many were equipped with one of two central types of pistol: the Makarov PM and the Stechkin APS. Both are 9mm pistols. The Makarov is a very compact pistol indeed, having an overall length of 160mm (6.3in). Its small size gives it a very low magazine capacity when compared to many other handguns – only eight rounds. Its operation is a straightforward blow-back type, and it features a double-action trigger and an external hammer. By contrast, the Stechkin is much larger – 225mm (8.9in) long and with a magazine capacity of a prodigious 20 rounds. The Stechkin actually strays towards the submachine category in some of its configurations. It can be fitted with a wooden stock and with modifications to the trigger mechanism it can fire full-automatic at a cyclical rate of 750rpm. This capability suggests why the backsights of the pistol can be adjusted from 25–200m (82–656ft). Pistols were generally part of the kit of Soviet officers, political troops or special forces, but pistols could occasionally be seen on the belts of NCOs, particularly when on active service in a region such as Afghanistan.

The final addition to the Soviet soldier's standard arsenal was a selection of hand grenades. Soviet hand grenades of the later 1970s were divided in four main types. By far the most common was the RDG-5, a cylindrical fragmentation grenade containing some 110g (3.85oz) of explosive which gave an effective fragmentation radius (EFR) of 25m (82ft). At 310gm (0.68lb) total weight, 114mm (4.5in) length and with a 3-4 second fuse delay the RDG5 is convenient to use and easy to carry in number. The RDG-5 replaced two other types of grenade, the RG42 and F-1. The latter closely resembles the British No.36 grenade with its segmented body of cast iron. It is usually distinguished from the British grenade by a long fuse protruding from the top of the body and also through its olive-drab paint. EFR of the F1 is 14.7m (47.24ft). In definite contrast to the F1 and RDG-5 is the cylindrical RG42, which has an appearance similar to the German stick grenade of World War II but without the long wooden handle. The HE charge of the RG42 is greater than the other fragmentation grenades – 118gm (4.16oz) – though its less effective design reduces the EFR when compared to the RDG5 to 20m (65.6ft). It also has a weight of 0.4kg (0.88lb), so is less easy to throw to distance. The final type of hand grenade found on Soviet personnel was the RKG3M anti-tank grenade, though this was not carried as a standard item of kit. Anti-tank grenades usually have a limited potential and require considerable accuracy in use, but the RKG3M could puncture about 127mm (5in) of armour. It accomplished this through a 0.567kg (1.25lb) charge behind a conical copper lining (this lining turns into a jet of molten particles upon explosion). The RKG-3M is thrown like a conventional grenade, but the pin deploys a small drogue parachute from the grenade's long wooden handle and this gives the grenade a straight nose-first flight pattern.

The combination of AK, pistol and grenades meant that the average Soviet infantryman had access to powerful personal firepower, and flexible response to various combat environments.

BOLT PROBLEMS

Bolt problems generally fall into two categories: either the bolt won't unlock or it won't lock. In both cases dirt on the bolt itself or down in the lug recesses is the most common cause and can be alleviated by field stripping, cleaning and lubrication. Failing that, the problem might lie in a faulty recoil spring or, more seriously, a damaged gas system. Effective locking will be impaired if the gas piston is damaged, loose or misaligned, or if the gas tube has been dented. In any of these cases, the primary repair procedure is to strip the gun down and replace the defective or damaged parts, not something that is generally easy to do in the field when spare gun parts are not usually carried. Thankfully for any combatant, the AK's bolt and gas system are especially rugged and their outright failure is rare.

FIRING PROBLEMS

Firing problems usually means that either the gun doesn't fire or, alarmingly when it occurs, the gun continues firing even after the trigger has been released. The latter problem is usually caused by a broken or soiled sear or trigger spring, and if a clean does not rectify the problem then parts may have to be replaced. At the opposite end of the scale, an AK that won't fire at all can indicate a much broader spectrum of troubles. For a start, it may not be the gun that is at fault but the ammunition – either the ammunition is of a poor quality or excessive oiling has led to some rounds becoming deactivated. Poor quality ammunition may also lead to the round not seating itself properly in the chamber, another cause of misfiring. The firing pin or hammer/hammer spring may also be dirty or broken and require cleaning/replacing. Finally, the bolt may not have seated itself in the full locked position, thus placing the firing pin out of reach of the round.

Having raised the problem of ammunition, it is worth AK users paying special attention to the origin of their rounds. AK ammunition is incredibly inexpensive, but a worldwide influx of ultra-cheap Chinese ammunition with corrosive primers and cases is causing many problems. If this ammunition is to be used, then cleaning must be extra diligent and increased in its frequency.

USAGE AND TRAINING

FEED PROBLEMS

If a simple check that the magazine is seated properly proves satisfactory, then almost all feed problems revolve around defective magazines or ammunition. If the magazine lips have been damaged, if dirt has entered the magazine space, or if the magazine spring has weakened, the end result is usually a misfeed or double-feed. Both these faults stop the weapon firing. In order to remedy this the magazine should be replaced with a fresh one or the soldier should clean out the existing magazine. A problem in feeding can also indicate difficulties with the gas action. Low-powered ammunition or damage to the gas-piston results in a lack of sufficient gas-pressure to cycle the action fully. As with other gas problems, the gas system should be dismantled and cleaned, or parts replaced if necessary.

EJECTION AND EXTRACTION PROBLEMS

Problems with the ejection of rounds from the AK47 tend to be associated with either a dirty ejector – in which case cleaning is required – or with a broken ejector, which needs replacing or repairing. More serious, however, are extraction problems. All cartridges expand upon firing against the walls of the chamber. The seal they make (called obduration) is necessary to prevent gas leakages out into the breech which would affect the operation of the bolt and create the risk of dangerous malfunction, as well as lessening the forward thrust behind the projectile. An extractor is required to draw the spent case to the ejection port. Usually a lack of extraction implies a broken extractor or a weak extractor spring – replacement of parts is necessary in both cases. Ammunition may also be at the root of the problem. Dirty or corrosive ammunition may have left build-ups on the extractor and in the chamber, both of which stop the smooth flow of the extractor system. Field stripping and thorough cleaning is required in this case. Finally, a weak and dirty recoil spring may be the cause of extraction problems by not allowing enough recoil action to give the extractor space to operate.

This list of potential problems is not exclusive, and different problems can produce different effects in other parts of the gun. Yet as this book has acknowledged, the AK rifles are some of the world's most reliable firearms, proven in battle. That experience of battle is the subject of the next chapter.

Below: Polish troops run through fire as part of battle training. Smoke can be a problem if allowed to make deposits in gun barrels, so good cleaning would be recommended after such an exercise.

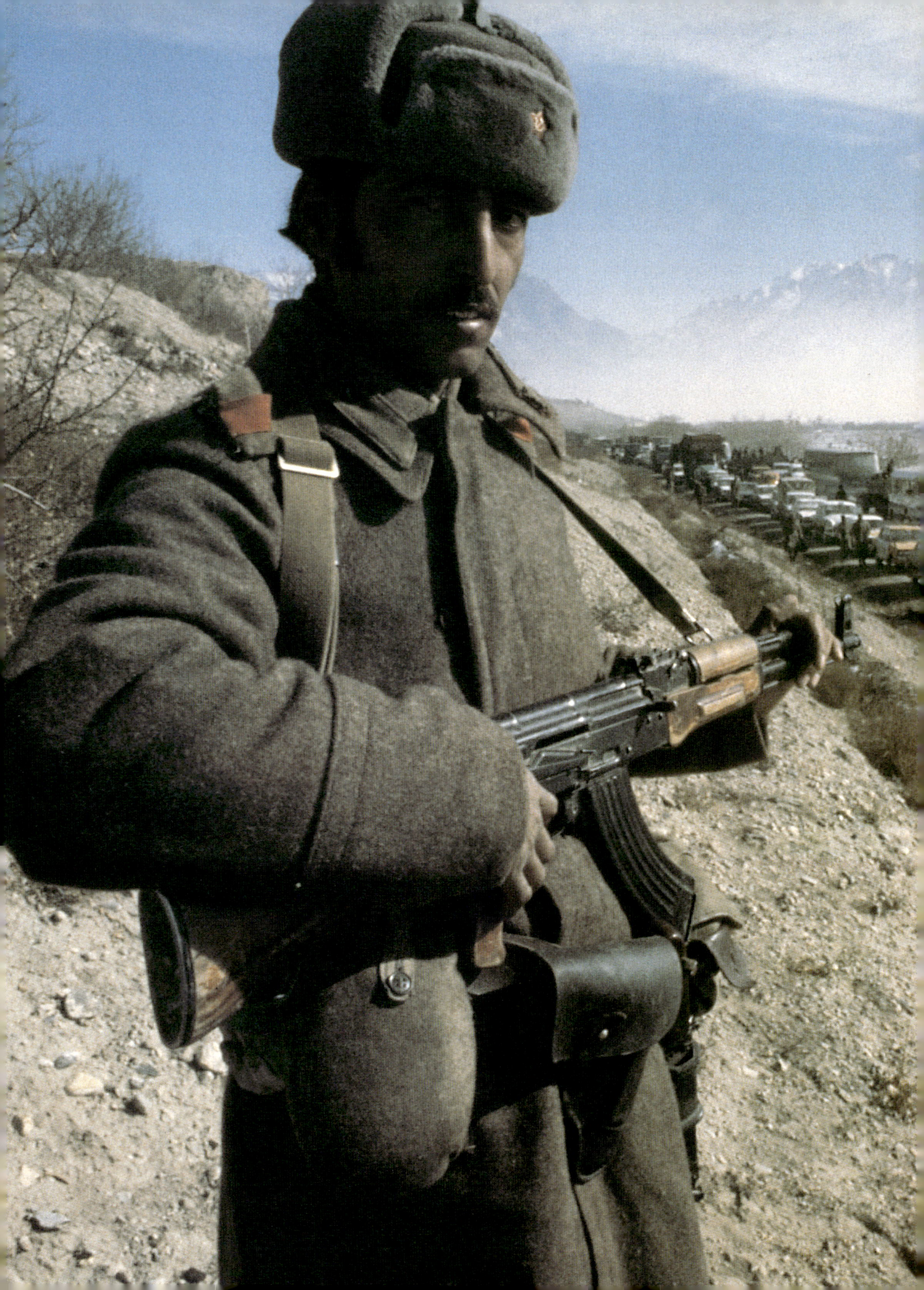

CHAPTER 4

Deployment and Battle

It is no exaggeration to say that one of the most pressing issues of world security today is the distribution of AK weapons. 80 million AK rifles are estimated to have been produced since the late 1940s; only a fraction of these are accounted for in regular armies.

The rest have been scattered across the face of the globe, selling for a few dollars in African markets, being shipped in bulk down through the Indian sub-continent, or appearing in the hands of South American insurgents. It might be argued that the trade in major weapons systems – such as tanks, medium-range missiles, and aircraft – is the real problem for world peace. Yet while these problems tend to affect political stability, which can turn into conflict, the trade in AKs actually results in the killing of thousands of people every year in all corners of the world.

In many countries today, the AK47 has now reached an almost iconic status. Large numbers of African males see the purchase of their first AK weapon as a true step into manhood and the membership certificate of a prestigious faction or group. Indeed, in South Africa during the apartheid era the AK stood out as a symbol of belonging to one of the anti-state parties, particularly the African National Congress. In turn, the South African government demonised the ANC by investing the AK with dark, almost satanic imagery in the publicity issued. Outside of Africa, this situation is repeated. In Northern Ireland both Republican and Loyalist terrorist groups paint murals featuring the AK in crossed sword-like patterns to symbolise armed defiance and military muscle. In Iraq, the massive street paintings of Saddam Hussein often feature him clasping an AK; the scene is frequently invested with a classical flavour and evokes the AK as the modern replacement for the knight's sword. Ironically, the AK has become an almost global symbol of both the massive formal power of communism and also the informal violence of terrorism.

Left: A Russian soldier watches over traffic during the Soviet occupation of Afghanistan. Many thousands of Russian soldiers here would be killed by the gun that emerged from their own homeland.

THE AK47

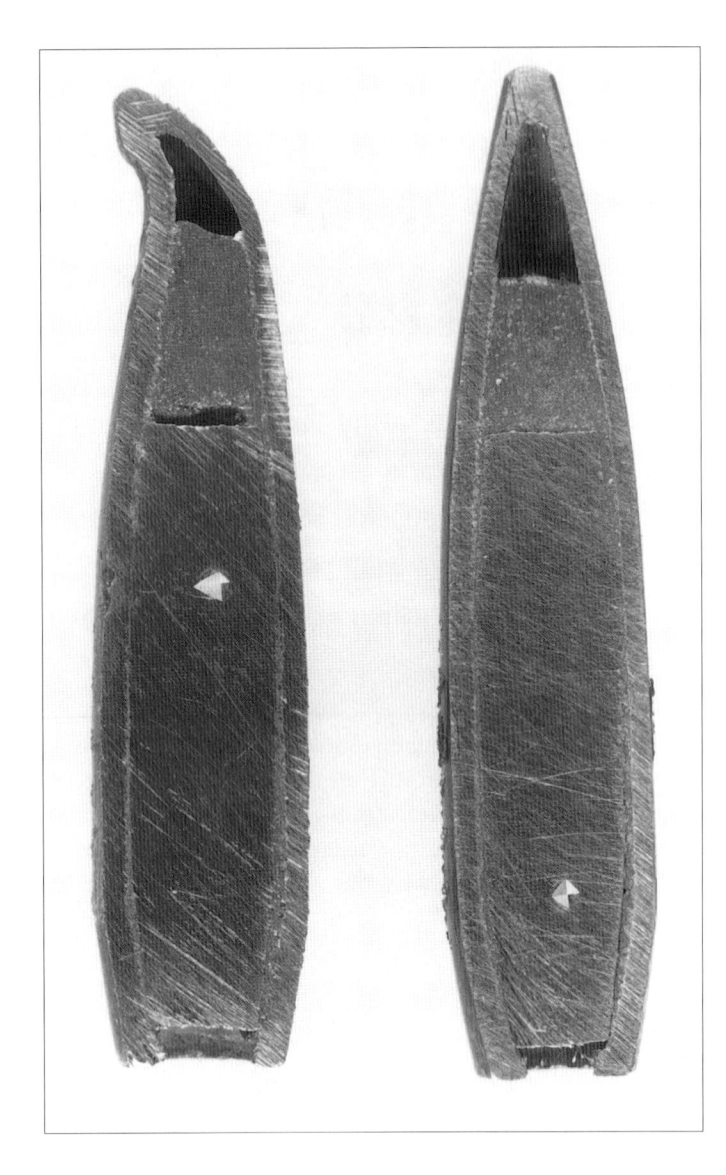

Above: A cross-sectional look at the 5.45mm round both before and after impact. Note how the cavity at the tip has caused the bullet to bend on impact, thus sending it tumbling through the victim.

This chapter will take an overview of how the AK47 has actually impacted on the world, looking at the facts behind its deployment, and examining the experience of using the weapon in battle and how it shaped up to other mainstream assault rifles. For in discussing any small arm the observer can become somewhat too focused on its technical qualities and performance. Of course, the primary objective of AK technology is to kill human beings. That the AK has achieved better than most other weapons large or small.

AMMUNITION AND EFFECTS

As unpalatable as it is, to understand the AK as a fighting weapon you have to understand what it can do to a human body. To do this, we will look at how the 7.62mm M43 intermediate round differs in ballistic results from the much smaller 5.45mm M74 round, and evaluate both in the context of the world-wide pursuit for the ideal combat round.

We have already explored the reasons for the development of the M43 in Chapter 1. Underlying them all, however, was the need for a cartridge that was controllable to use but which could put down a person effectively and powerfully. Full-power rifle cartridges had great penetrative ability, perhaps too much. If a rifle bullet passes straight through a person and keeps a clean line of flight then in ballistic terms a lot of its take-down energy is exerted towards exiting the victim and maintaining the flight. The ideal for an effective bullet is for all of its energy to be transferred into the victim, thus hitting the victim with the full ballistic force available.

The M43 round approached this ideal. Initially, Soviet armourers set the competition to design an intermediate cartridge with the criteria that it should retain 196 joules of residual energy at 600m (1968ft), enough for it to penetrate 225mm (8.8in) of pine boards. This would give a good penetrative ability while channelling more energy into target impact. During firing trails it was found that when it impacted upon the target, the M43 tended to follow a fairly straight line through the body without fragmentation but tumbled head over tail to open up larger cavities on its way through (the bullet would drop quickly to the ground after exiting). The net result was good killing performance. Full-power rifle rounds such as the 7.62 x 51mm NATO also spun in the victim, but the force of the bullet made a narrow single track before exiting forcefully rather than the multiple cavities of the M43.

Taken in an overall view, the M43 made the AK47 and AKM rifles potent combat tools in most practical environments. A burst of four or five rounds from an AK, accurately positioned, would create a terrible range of tissue damage, and the tumbling effect of the rounds within the body cavity meant the bullets made an irregular course through the human bone, muscle and tissue. The lethality of the M43 had to be retained as the shift to smaller calibre rounds took place in the late 1960s and 1970s. Small calibre rounds have their reduced calibre compensated for by the high velocities at which they are fired. The effect of being hit by a high-velocity (around 1000mps/3048fps) round is in essence the same as that achieved by hurling a rock forcibly into a pond. Human cells are some 75 per cent water. When the enormous supersonic force of a high-velocity round passes through the human body, 'ripples' are sent through this water content by the accompanying shock wave – known as 'hydrostatic shock'. As this occurs massive tissue damage results. A US Marine Sergeant has recounted his shock in the Vietnam war when he first hit a Vietcong insurgent with a burst from his 5.56mm M16. He fired off three rounds. The first two peppered the floor at the feet of the enemy soldier.

Right: US Special Forces soldiers place demolition charges on a bridge support. The soldier on the left is armed with the non-US AK rifle – the ubiquity of this gun makes it essential for elite units to master its principles.

DEPLOYMENT AND BATTLE

AK47

The last round, however, hit the man in the shoulder. According the US soldier the Vietcong man's arm was taken completely off at the shoulder and his whole body was thrown so hard at the ground the unfortunate man bounced into the air. Not surprisingly, he was dead from shock within a matter of seconds.

This story bears out tests conducted on the 5.56 x 45mm bullet. The permanent cavity left by the bullet tends to be enormous, and in addition the bullet fragments and sends lead and steel splinters throughout the victim. So how does the 5.45mm M74 compare as used in the Soviet AK74? The velocity is about the same, so heavy hydrostatic shock is imparted. Yet the M74 has a different destructive action. The tip of the M74 is empty and the weight is set well back toward the rear of the round. On impact, the hollow tip crumples, thus destabilising the bullet and allowing the rear weight to flip forward. Once this occurs then bullet tumbling is increased even more than the M43. Indeed, despite the smaller calibre both the temporary and permanent cavities left by the M74 are larger than those imparted by its larger relative.

In effect the AK47, AKM and AK74 are refined killing tools of the highest order. The AK74, for example, has such controllable recoil that a soldier could easily maintain a stream of 10-15 of these vicious rounds into a man-sized target. It is readily apparent why the distribution of AK weapons has become an issue of world-wide concern.

COMBAT ADVANTAGES

Before going on to chart more of how the AK rifles have been and are being distributed, it is worth taking an overview of why the AK is such a popular weapon to use. There are literally hundreds of small arms in the world today available through regular and irregular markets, so why is it that the AK is so desirable? It must be admitted from the outset that one of the key reasons for the AK's popularity is that it is cheap and it is out there in large numbers. This issue will be addressed shortly, but first the experiences of the weapon's operator, the soldier, should be considered.

In terms of battlefield performance, the strength of the AK rifles separate out into three main qualities: controllable firepower, durability, and ease of maintenance. These issues should be taken in order. A typical AKM rifle imparts about 7.19 joules of recoil force through the butt plate upon firing. This is a manageable recoil force, especially as the gun is fairly compact, and it enables a practical rate of fire to approach around 100rpm and a practical range of up to 300m (984ft). In firing range tests, a soldier trained in the use of the AK47 was able to develop a grouping of 101-152mm (4-6in) at a distance of 100m (328ft). This is an excellent practical

DEPLOYMENT AND BATTLE

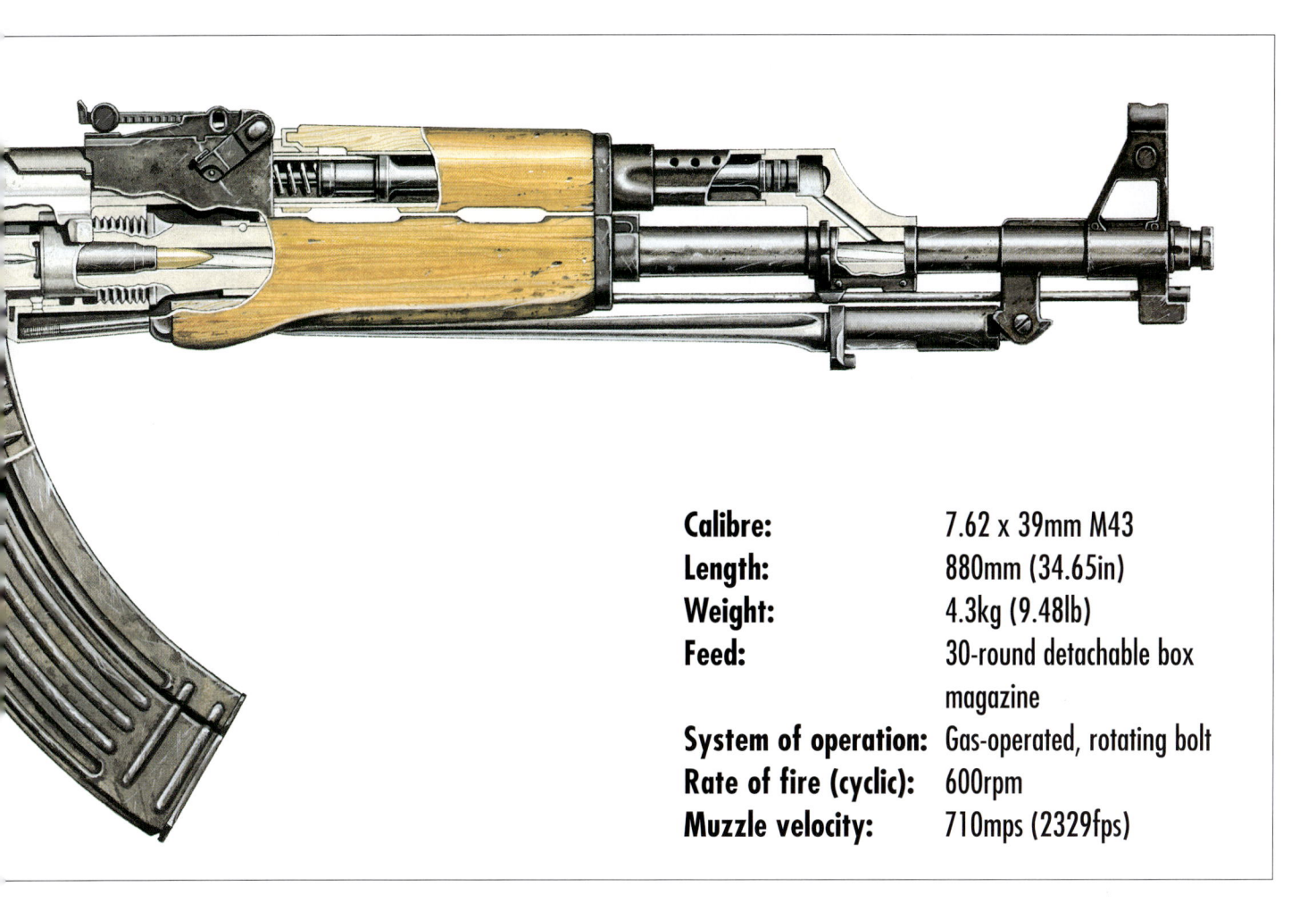

Calibre: 7.62 x 39mm M43
Length: 880mm (34.65in)
Weight: 4.3kg (9.48lb)
Feed: 30-round detachable box magazine
System of operation: Gas-operated, rotating bolt
Rate of fire (cyclic): 600rpm
Muzzle velocity: 710mps (2329fps)

grouping for combat, as generally the aiming point is the centre of the torso to increase the probability of a hit, and a hit on a vital organ. The AKM showed an even greater degree of accuracy because of its rate-reducing hammer-delay which allowed the soldier more steady bursts. Accuracy was also helped on the AKM by the angular muzzle compensator.

With the introduction of the AK74 the potential for accurate killing increased exponentially. The target-shooting figures are impressive. At a distance of 200m (656ft), an AK74 in good hands was quite capable of 152mm (6in) groupings. Throw the range out to 800m (2624ft) and 203–254mm (8–10in) groupings were attained – still a very lethal pattern for torso-aimed shots. The main reasons for this controllability are the reduction in recoil force – the AK74 imparts only 3.39 joules of recoil to the butt – and the very effective muzzle-brake/compensator. Tests in the US show that with the muzzle fitting on, the groupings are tight around the centre of the target at 25m (82ft) from a continuous 30-round burst. Remove the muzzle fitting and the pattern goes very loose, wide and random.

East German studies of all the AK weapons produced a breakdown of hit probabilities in light of the changes in calibre in the AK weapons. For the AK47/AKM, 300m (984ft) range produced a hit probability of 29 per cent. Take that up to 400m (1312ft) and the hit probability drops to around 16 per cent. These are still respectable figures, but the contrast with the AK74 is great. Taking the 300m (984ft) mark again as our base line, the AK74's hit probability rises to 40 per cent, and at 400m (1312ft) 25 per cent. But accuracy is not the only difference between the two calibres of weapon. The East German military also made judgements about kill probabilities – this was based on two rounds hitting the target and the potential for more lethal accuracy. Getting hit by two 7.62mm rounds from an AK47 at 300m (984ft) results in a 50 per cent likelihood of your death. At 400m (1312ft) that figure drops to 40 per cent. However, with the AK74 300m (984ft) generates a 64 per cent kill probability and 400m (1312ft) a 43 per cent probability.

These figures tell us that as an all-round combat weapon the AK74 has a marked advantage over the AK47/AKM. Yet the criteria of what makes a good weapon is not entirely about the handling during fire. The AK47 and AKM may be less accurate and have less killing force than the AK74, but in actual fighting they have still proved themselves lethal firearms. Another reason for this is that they keep on firing when other guns fail.

Reliability counts for a great deal in an infantry weapon. In a firefight, the consequences of a gun jamming are frequently lethal as the firer is left exposed and his attention is diverted by trying to clear the jam and repair the failing. This

THE AK47

dirt without failing. The chrome-lined barrel is durable and does not easily wear out. Its furniture is tough. The whole design of the weapon tends towards simplicity, resulting in less to go wrong.

What this all meant for the combat soldier was that in action sustained fire could be maintained without the gun malfunctioning or losing its performance. As long as it was occasionally field-stripped and cleaned, the AK would go on and on. Such reliability breeds confidence in the soldier, and once a soldier is confident in his weaponry then he tends to perform better in battle (see current British experiences with the undependable SA80 for a negative illustration).

The AK rifle is also very easy to maintain. This may seem as something removed from the actual combat use of the gun, but in fact it is integral to efficient fighting usage. During battle, moments of rest are precious and any gun that is laborious to maintain will soon be neglected. Such neglect will express itself in an unreliable gun. Furthermore, in an emergency situation when a gun fails, quick field-stripping action means that you can amend a problem in seconds while covering-fire is provided. Cadets of the Komsomol in Russia are expected to be able to field-strip an AK rifle in a mere 30 seconds. This means that a full strip, clean and reassembly can be accomplished in about two minutes if under exceptional pressure.

The combination of firepower, reliability and ease of maintenance come together in a weapon that is not the most sophisticated, but it will be the last one shooting after other guns have failed. Hence it is instantly understandable why the AK had achieved such popularity – people will trust their lives with very few pieces of engineering. Yet the other major factor in the success story of the AK, and its massive contribution to the post-war battlefield, is simply that is was there. As has been already noted, some 80 million AKs litter the world. They are incredibly easy for countries to manufacture under licence, and for dealers from the illegal arms trade to obtain. So what is the pattern of distribution of AK rifles around the world? And what is the impact to the society of those countries? From this overview of deployment, three illustrations of the AK's combat contribution in three very different wars, will be considered: the Vietnam War, the Arab-Israeli conflict of the 1967, and the Soviet invasion and occupation of Afghanistan.

LICENSED MANUFACTURE AND AUTHORISED DISTRIBUTION

The AK47 was not a gun destined to stay within Soviet borders. The Cold War had formed East and West into huge opposing camps, and there was a demand on both sides for there to be common weapons to aid in the combined might of the stand off. As a rule, the countries which made up the

Above: Chinese troops practise their bayonet drill. China's AK47 copy – the Type 56 – went on to become one of the most prolific AK variants. It appeared on battlefields from Southeast Asia to Africa.

was made particularly apparent in the early years of the Vietnam War (see below) when US M16 rifles jammed in action because of carbon build-up in the gas-systems. With the AK rifles, the soldier will have few such concerns. During the testing phases of AK development the prototype weapons alone stood up to incredible abuse. They were used in freezing weather, fired after being underwater, buried in mud and sand and left for days just to be dug up, cocked and fired as normal.

The essence of the AK's reliability remains in several factors. The rotational locking of the bolt is very solid indeed, and can easily tolerate the ingress of quantities of

Right: A soldier from the Chinese navy stands guard with his Type 56 held firm. Note the integral triangular-blade folding bayonet which was standard fitment on the Chinese weapons.

DEPLOYMENT AND BATTLE

Warsaw Pact had less financial virility than the Western alliance. This, combined with the need to supply the armies with competent assault rifles, led quickly to widespread acceptance of the AK47 as a common weapon. The AK was cheap to make and buy, was impressive in combat, and would be provided with extensive Soviet assistance either in constructing production facilities or in monetary subsidies. It is very difficult in this present time to ascertain the full picture about AK distribution and licensed manufacture. Partly this is because actual records are scarce, and partly because once other countries started to make AKs then they in turn either supplied to others or helped them make their own. For example, in the late 1950s China began making its own version of the AK47, the Type 56. This in turn has been sent out to countries ranging from North Korea and Vietnam to Gabon and Somalia in Africa. In the process the numbers of manufacture and the destinations to which they were deployed get incredibly muddied. Part of the reason why there is so much concern about AK rifles today is that the vast majority of them are unaccounted for in any official way. The issue of illegal arms trading will be covered in a moment, but first all we can do is give a brief run through of what we know about the state of production of the AK in countries other than the Soviet Union.

Below: A Croatian soldier lets off a stream of 5.45mm rounds from his AK74 rifle. The controllability of the AK74 owing to its low recoil makes it lethally accurate, even on full auto.

China has been one of the biggest producers of AK-type weapons in the world. During the 1950s the Soviet Union engaged with the Chinese to help them establish their own AK production facilities. The result was that by the 1960s Type 56 assault rifles were being produced in large numbers not only to equip the Chinese Army, but also for various export markets. The Vietnam War provided one of the biggest catalysts for Type 56 distribution, and it should be remembered that AK weapons pictured in the hands of Vietcong guerrillas are more often than not of Chinese origin. Yet further exports went to places far way from the Far East. Albania, for instance, received heavy caches of Type 56 weapons during its communist history, and the Sudan was one of China's major export markets for assault rifles. Apart from this type of export, the numbers of Type 56s involved are apparent if the size of China's army is considered – a total manpower of about 10 million troops (three million regular and five to seven million reservists). Factor in exports and replacement weapons and an estimated of 15–20 million AKs produced is feasible.

China was helped in its production of the AK47 because of general communist affiliation (an affiliation which broke down steadily through the 1970s and 80s), but the Warsaw Pact provided a more immediate context for the extension of Soviet AK distribution. The primary players in this scenario were East Germany (known as the German Democratic Republic), Poland, Romania, Bulgaria, Hungary with North Korea and the former Yugoslavia being non-Pact beneficiaries

Above: The AK rifle shown here is fitted with a laser-training device: a low-powered laser beam instead of a bullet is fired, allowing the user safely to register hits on live people.

of Soviet assistance. Between them these countries account for many millions of internally-produced AK weapons, and many millions transported across the world to various countries and regimes. East Germany itself produced up to two million AK-type weapons and opened up substantial export markets in African and Middle Eastern countries. Poland has produced a similar number of AK firearms, mainly the standard PMK assault rifle. Poland was also one of the earliest countries outside of the Soviet Union to start producing weapons on behalf of another Warsaw Pact member. Bulgaria's first AK weapons were actually made entirely in Poland, before it started to build its own production facilities (the transitional period was handled with Poland supplying AK parts for straightforward assembly in Bulgaria). Other than Bulgaria, Poland's AK weapons spread widely, particularly in the Middle East.

Hungary, Bulgaria and Romania were somewhat smaller producers of the AK, though they have still turned out large numbers of the weapons between them, about two million. These weapons have spread fairly broadly across the world, particularly to Africa and the Middle East. Warsaw Pact countries were amazingly deep repositories of weapons supply in the 1960s–80s, mainly because they were willing sponsors of world-wide communist military effort and also because they were keen to raise hard cash. Weapons from these three countries in particular have appeared in a broad sweep of nations and contexts. Algeria, Congo, the Caribbean, Nicaragua and Syria are typical examples.

Still within the communist parameter, the former Yugoslavia and North Korea are producers of some 4–5 million weapons, North Korea accounting for two-thirds of that output. Whereas Yugoslavian weapons tended to stay more within their own borders, those produced by North Korea went in large numbers into the Middle East and Africa – by no coincidence two areas that have suffered more than most from AK proliferation. Outside of the Warsaw Pact and communist affiliates, there are a number of other countries such as Finland and Israel who have not so much produced their own AKs as produced variants modified for their own national use. With these added – and the numbers run to several million – the picture of AK distribution around the world is one of massive industry. While many countries were producing their own AKs and the Soviet Union was distributing millions abroad to various sympathetic regimes, the world became more enmeshed in a problem of unauthorised distribution. AK-related violence has spread from the

57

Above: Here two Middle Eastern gunmen show off an RPG weapon and an AK rifle. Armed terrorism and guerrilla violence has been made infinitely more possible by the distribution of Kalashnikovs.

comprehensible hands of soldiers into a bewildering range of criminal, insurgent and factional groups. This is supported by the illegal arms trade, now potentially the biggest distribution route for AK rifles.

AKS AND THE ILLEGAL ARMS TRADE

Along with 9mm pistols, AK rifles are the dominant currency in the world's illegal arms trade. The scale of the problem is enormous. Increases in criminal violence, guerrilla wars and terrorist acts have all been linked to the availability of AKs, spread as they were across the world by Cold War conflicts, foreign manufacture and illicit deals.

One of the fundamental reasons for the AK problem is their incredible cheapness on the international market, a cheapness achieved by their prolific manufacture and their easy availability. The AK has become so cheap that in Russia criminal hit-men often leave an AK on the body of their victim as a form of calling card. In Central Asia, an AK will cost around $100 to buy, actually expensive compared to many nations. Africa is awash with AKs, and one can be bought in a place such as Mozambique for $6 or even as a swap for a bag of maize. In South Africa, Namibia and Angola the figure varies between R.50 and R.1500 (South Africa is the more expensive nation because of tighter border controls and better policing).

Such inexpense, combined with the fact that such arms are easily accessible has led to terrible consequences. In South Africa, deaths by shooting increased from 688 in 1991 to 966 in 1992 following an influx of AKs into the country. Similar stories have been told throughout Africa, the Indian subcontinent and even many Eastern European nations – the war in the former Yugoslavia saw major transfers of AKs into the country to fuel the conflict. So what are the world-wide routes by which AKs are passed around? These will be examined region by region.

EUROPE AND THE FORMER SOVIET UNION

The territories of the former Soviet Union are a natural place to start our overview of the trade in illegal AKs. With the collapse of the Soviet Union, the regulations over Warsaw Pact firearms dissolved and it became increasingly difficult to track where the rifles were going. Simultaneously, the economic downturn in the fortunes of many peoples in the CIS meant that arms became an ideal method of income generation.

Right: A US officer from the US and Caribbean security forces displays a crate of AK47 assault rifles discovered on the island of Grenada during the conflict between the two countries in 1983.

DEPLOYMENT AND BATTLE

THE AK47

Above: Africa has been one of the biggest recipients of Cold War and blackmarket AK weaponry. Here Eritrean child guerrillas perform drills with wooden guns carved in an unmistakable shape.

Millions of AKs are thus spread across a vast territory with poor accounting. Consequently the former Soviet Union acts almost like the hub of an arms-trade wheel, feeding thousands upon thousands of AKs out into world.

Much of this illegal trade is done by military personnel themselves. In 1993 alone, over 3000 Russian army officers were found to have been involved in illegal arms dealing. Their primary customers are the criminals of the Russian underworld, these either using the weapons themselves or more commonly passing them on to more major arms dealers in places like Prague. Prague itself is classed as the capital of illegal AK trading (indeed trading in all Eastern Bloc weaponry), while the Ukraine also trades weapons heavily with Europe, Asia and the Middle East. A major customer for the AK in recent years has been the Balkans, undoubtedly aiding the escalation of war in the former Yugoslavia, and also the Middle East and South Asia. In addition, the collapse of the Albanian government in 1993 led to the massive looting of AK weaponry from state arsenals by criminal groups. This theft is estimated to have injected up to one million weapons

Left: Soldiers fighting in Guinea in 1972 stop for a period to clean their weapons. In Africa the AK is incredibly cheap; it can even be bought as a swap for a bag of maize in some countries.

into the illegal arms trade, the vast majority of them AK firearms. Even the UK has not been immune – Chinese and Soviet AKs have turned up in criminal activity in Manchester and are used heavily by terrorist organisations in Northern Ireland.

Until there is greater accountability for weapons in the former Soviet Union, and until army officers are paid more than mere subsistence, the problems in AK traffic will continue.

ASIA

The main problem areas in Asia for AK trafficking are Southeast Asia and South Asia. In Southeast Asia, many of the illegal firearms are US manufactured because of the caches left over after the Vietnam War – 946,000 M16A1 rifles were left behind when the US forces departed there in 1975. These spread around the Philippines and Thailand, and feed the spiralling violence of piracy, murder and kidnapping. The AK also makes its contribution mainly through distribution of Chinese Type 56 weapons. Many of these were used during the Vietnam War but China also has several major illegal arms bazaars which export Chinese AKs widely. Customers for Type 56 weapons are as diverse as Albania and the Sudan, but even the US has been targeted – some 2000 Type 56s were intercepted in the process of being illegally imported.

In South Asia, however, the problem is a lot more acute. The central reason for this problem is the Soviet invasion of Afghanistan in 1979 and its subsequent nine-year occupation. During the occupation, not only were thousands of AKs seized by Afghan guerrillas who used them to fight with and to raise funds through trading, but the US sponsored massive arms transfers via Pakistan into the country as part of its support for the anti-Soviet forces. During this time $8 billion of arms were sent in through Pakistan, and the head of Pakistan's Inter-Service Intelligence Agency has confirmed that three million AKs were stocked for distribution on the Pakistan-Afghan border. Consequently, Afghanistan, Pakistan, India and Sri Lanka became awash with AK weaponry on a huge scale. The consequences have been an appalling history of factional violence and crime – even feuds between families have resulted in AK battles such is the widespread distribution of the gun. With millions of guns scattered throughout the country, the prospects for political stability in the region are fraught with the burden of easily available firepower.

Below: US Rangers during the operation on Grenada in 1983 display a hoard of captured weapons, mainly AK47s and AKMs. The machine gun on the far right is a Czech M52/57.

AFRICA

Perhaps more than any other world region, Africa is blighted by the presence of AKs. The Cold War conflicts that were fought across Africa by proxy during the 1960s–80s meant that communist arms flooded into the continent. Almost every country in Africa received Soviet or Warsaw Pact light weapons during this period. Additionally, Cuba played a significant role in distributing the AK. Ethiopia, for example, received military aid from the Soviet Union and also some 9000 Cuban troops during its war with Somalia in the 1970s. Thus not only did the Ethiopians receive arms from Soviet suppliers, the Cubans also left their AKs behind when they departed.

Such is the extent of the distribution of AKs in Africa that China has even built a factory manufacturing 7.62 x 39mm rounds in Uganda. (The African market is good considering that the Angolan government made purchases of four million AK rounds in the early 1990s.) The Chinese venture is not surprising considering that countries such as Mozambique alone received up to one million AKs from the Soviet Union, though this is only a fraction of the six million AKs which fill the country. Similar stories are told through Africa, and the consequences have been hideous. Much of the slaughter of the some 250,000 Tutsi people in Rwanda in 1993-94 was conducted with AKs bought directly by the Hutu government from Russia. 50-60,000 people in Liberia still carry AKs, and the country is a victim of meaningless violence on the scale of war. Gangs of thrill-seeking killers murder every day with AKs throughout Africa, and it is now customary to see alarming pictures of children as young as six years old staggering under the weight of an AK rifle. Because of the AK's very reliability, Africa's AKs will dog its road to economic recovery for decades to come.

LATIN AMERICA

Latin America has had significant problem with arms trafficking just like the regions above, yet in this case most of the weapons are of US origin. The US is a naturally more adjacent source of weaponry than the Eastern Bloc, and the US sponsorship of various military groups in South American conflicts has meant the widespread presence of US M14 and M16 rifles. However, this situation has far from excluded the AK rifle. Cuba was one major exception to the arms trade pattern of Latin America, receiving as it did large-scale supplies of Eastern Bloc weapons to support its communist independence. In turn, Chile benefited from Cuban weapon supplies, and it is not uncommon to find AKs cropping up in almost all Latin American countries in varying numbers.

The profile of AK world-wide distribution that has just been discussed indicates why so many of the world's coun-

Below: This Rangers scout on patrol in Vietnam is armed with an AK. This was a common choice made by US soldiers in Vietnam, as the AK often provided greater reliability than the US M16.

DEPLOYMENT AND BATTLE

Right: A Viet Cong soldier is pictured here carrying little more than his AK47 and ammunition pouches. The pouches are worn across the chest in a style typical of the communist soldiers of East Asia.

tries are known as 'weaponised societies'. Kalashnikov's invention put cheap guns into the hands of millions – soldiers and civilians. On a local level, the world is essentially a more unstable place because of the AK47, and there must be many countries in the world whose citizens are continually haunted by the appearance of that distinctive curved magazine. Our focus now, however, turns to how the AK has actually been used in conventional battle. As a landmark weapon, it is right to explore how individual conflicts have been shaped by its presence. This is not an easy issue. The relevance of common rifles is rarely discussed or charted in post-battle analysis open to public access. Yet a good approach would be to see how the AK47 contributed to three different conflicts in particular – the Vietnam War, the Arab-Israeli Six-Day War in 1967, and the Mujahideen's resistance to Soviet occupation in Afghanistan in the 1980s. These three conflicts are representative of the AK47 because they show the gun in three different climates and terrains and clearly set the AK against the other weapons that distinguished themselves in the twentieth century.

THE VIETNAM WAR

The Vietnam War brought the AK47 to the attention of the West more than any other event. Indeed the AK came to symbolise the communist cause almost as much as the hammer and sickle itself. Press agencies published pictures of Vietcong guerrillas dressed in civilian clothes, conical straw hats and wearing shoes cut from vehicle types, and carrying a crude-looking weapon with a pronounced curved magazine. In most cases this gun was not strictly an AK47 but more likely a Chinese Type 56, as China was a central supplier of small arms to North Vietnam between 1963 and 1975. Yet the gun seemed to represent the unsophisticated strength of the Vietcong and NVA. Newspaper columns spoke of the legendary reliability of the weapon, the implication being that the AK-armed guerrilla would be a durable foe for US troops in Vietnam.

Yet those who knew best about the effect of the AK47 were the US soldiers in the field. With a high rate of fire, the AK could create the most horrifying ambush. Three Vietcong soldiers could dispense 90 rounds of 7.62mm ammunition into a US patrol in about four seconds, leaving behind them bodies appallingly injured by the AK's tumbling rounds. However, what made the conflict more distinctive than most in its use of small arms was that it seemed to bring into conflict two weapons which delineated the different approaches to and ideologies of the war – the AK and the US M16A1.

The M16 was a very different animal to the AK47. It had steadily replaced the 7.62mm M14 rifle as the standard US

Above: Two Soviet soldiers on convoy protection in Afghanistan. One is armed with an AGS 17 automatic grenade launcher while his colleague prepares to put down suppressing fire from his AK74.

infantry weapon by 1967 and demonstrated weapons development at its most sophisticated for the time. Much of the construction utilised plastics to create a lightweight firearm of 2.86kg (6.3lb). Its 5.56mm round, as has been already noted, had a gruesome killing power at ranges beyond those of the AK. Though both guns shared a rotating-bolt gas operation, the AK was undeniably more basic in construction at almost every level. Yet in combat, the sophistication of the M16 did not yield any exceptional advantage over the AK. In fact, the M16's advanced technology almost proved its undoing in combat with the AK.

During the early years of the Vietnam war, the M16 had an unfortunate tendency to jam in combat. By contrast, the AK rarely jammed regardless of environmental condition or firing demands. This led to some disparity in combat effectiveness. The problem with the M16 was that it was not initially designed for the standard US propellant, and carbon deposits tended to build up in the chamber and thus stop the bolt extracting a spent round. Soldiers started to die because of this problem, and even a US Congressional Committee investigated the matter. Though the essential problem was eventually remedied by chroming the chamber and improving the ammunition, the first stage of rectification was ensuring that the gun was regularly maintained and cleaned (in the early years of the war there was a shortage of cleaning equipment because of the rush to supply soldiers with weapons). This was easier said than done in the field, especially on some of the long 'Search and Destroy' operations the US conducted between 1965 and 1968. Soldiers would spend exhausting days patrolling through the dense jungle and suffocating Vietnamese heat. Thus when periods of rest were taken, the first thought was not weapons maintenance but relaxation and food.

By contrast, the Vietcong had a weapon that even in the corrosive jungle climate needed minimal maintenance. Many US soldiers started to use captured AKs because of the exceptional reliability they offered. Yet there were some problems for the Vietcong in using the AK47. One of these was the issue of fire discipline. Having been used to old French weapons for many years, the Vietcong had to adjust to a weapon that could empty its magazine in seconds. The issue was of concern to Vietcong and NVA leaders because ammunition supply was not always consistent, especially when ammunition convoys had been bombed on the Ho Chi Minh trail.

Thus Communist trainers had to teach their soldiers good fire discipline and also ensure that supplies were there when needed. A common approach was to have a fixed, hidden ammunition site which would be used after an ambush rather than transporting large quantities of ammunition into the field. For example, the VC 514th Battalion operating in Dinh Tuong province in the Mekong Delta would go en masse to resupply at a central arms dump after a significant action. The process would take about one day because of the

DEPLOYMENT AND BATTLE

need to hide from US surveillance, but once rearmed they would recommence their active duties.

It is impossible to say which weapon 'won' the day in Vietnam, as much of a weapon's capabilities is in the hands of its operator. What did become clear to the West, however, was that the basic AK was more than an equal for the expensive M16 in confined jungle conditions.

THE SIX-DAY WAR – 1967

The 'Six-Day War' which occurred when Israel launched an attack against Egypt, Jordan and Syria on 5 June 1967 was a defining moment in the application of weapons technology. Israel's airforce of modern jets made a blitzkrieg-style attack which in only a few hours wiped out the airborne opposition, most of the Arab aircraft being destroyed before they even left the ground. British-made Centurion V tanks and Soviet-made T-54s fought in the desert while the West watched intently this apparent rehearsal for potential Soviet/NATO tank battles of the future. But is was also a defining moment for Israel in terms of its small arms technology. For the Six-Day War brought it into contact with the AK.

During the 1950s Israel had managed to standardise its inconsistent rifle armoury in favour of the internationally popular FN FAL. This 7.62 x 51mm NATO calibre rifle was strong, simple, very reliable and very powerful. Its killing range extended well over a mile – especially in the desert regions of the Middle East where day-time air resistance is much less than that found in more European latitudes. Undoubtedly the FN FAL was and is a fine weapon, and to this day over 70 countries have used it as their standard self-loading rifle. Yet for the Israelis in 1967, the AK encounter would change their thinking.

Though people now tend to think of the Six-Day War as a battle conducted in wide-open desert spaces, that is far from the case. Fighting was conducted in Egyptian towns such as El Arish and Port Said, and the mountainous Golan Heights saw deeply entrenched Syrian troops having to be winkled out of well-constructed defensive positions. In these situa-

Below: During the Yom Kippur conflict of 1973, Egyptian soldiers brandish their AK rifles in defiance of the Israeli forces. The experience of AK firepower led Israel to a rethink of their small arms.

tions, the FN FAL started to display its disadvantages. It was long (1053mm/41.46in) and heavy 4.3kg (9.5), two factors which made it both unwieldy in confined spaces and exhausting to carry in the suffocating desert heat. By contrast, the Arab armies were mainly equipped with AK47s and AKMs, both convenient to carry, move and shoot from trenches and buildings. It also had the advantage that its low recoil made it easier to shoot with accuracy, whereas the FALs potent kick meant that bursts of fire tended to lose their accuracy. Moreover, the AK was quite capable of spraying out automatic fire in dense patterns, whereas the FAL was fixed at semi-automatic only.

The meeting of these two weapons awakened the Israeli authorities to the deficiencies in their small-arms selection. AK firepower had shown the truth of assessments that German officers had made back in the 1930s – practical combat range is under 300m (984ft) and performance over those ranges was best confined to sniper rifles and machine guns. Both weapons were reliable under the sandy conditions of battle, but the long-range firepower of the FAL was of questionable relevance even in the open spaces of the Sinai desert – heat haze in desert regions tends to prevent accurate long-range aiming once the cool early morning period has passed.

Thus it was that in the aftermath of the Six-Day War the Israelis developed the Galil rifle as a replacement for the FAL. The Galil was effectively a Kalashnikov variant (copied from the Finnish Valmet) except in 5.56mm calibre. The Israeli's experience of the AK's sound combat principles had altered their perception of what was needed from an infantry rifle. Their copying of the AK is one of the most complimentary recognitions that Kalashnikov had designed a true fighter's weapon.

AFGHANISTAN 1979–89

The Soviet occupation of Afghanistan is interesting for our AK story because both sides were armed with the same assault rifles, but employed them with very different tactics. When the Soviets invaded Afghanistan in 1979 in an attempt to prop up a flagging pro-Soviet regime, they were faced by a loose but extensive collection of guerrilla warriors, known collectively as the Mujahideen. These were fearsome if initially unsophisticated warriors, most of them armed with weapons from the days of British imperial influence such as the .303in Lee Enfield.

Such long-range firearms had their use in Afghanistan's mountainous terrain – Mujahideen guerrillas could snipe at Soviet convoys from high up the mountains before disap-

Left: Mujahideen guerrillas display their AKM rifles. AKs were acquired by the Mujahideen either by capturing them from the Soviets or from massive CIA-sponsored supplies through Pakistan.

pearing into their familiar terrain. Yet in pitched combat, the guerrillas' bolt-action firearms were no match for the ranks of AKs wielded by the Soviets. Though the dominant Soviet tactic in Afghanistan avoided close-quarter fighting – helicopter gunships and artillery were used against the Afghans in the mountains – many thousands of Soviet Spetsnaz Special forces did seek out Mujahideen bases and engage in firefights. The effects of these raids could be devastating. Armed with AKs, the Spetsnaz soldiers would pick off the guerrillas with rapid streams of automatic fire even as the Mujahideen attempted to operate their antiquated rifles.

Yet the situation changed. The US started to back the Afghan resistance movement and, ironically, AK arms started to pour across the border from Pakistan and into the hands of the Mujahideen. Slowly, the disparity in arms started to close, and special forces operations were steadily curtailed as the operations became increasingly dangerous. The Soviets reverted to more cautious operations. The standard Soviet operation consisted of driving tanks and APCs against Mujahideen positions under the cover of artillery and helicopter gunships, usually resulting in the guerrillas fleeing and the Soviets performing a scorched-earth policy in their wake.

The Mujahideen knew that a full engagement with armour and aircraft would be suicidal. Yet with AKs increasingly in their hands they could adopt a new strategy of attrition. They perfected the ambush. Afghanistan is a very mountainous country intertwined by narrow valleys and roads. Soviet supply convoys slavishly had to follow these routes despite their vulnerability. The Mujahideen tactic was to start a land-slide to block the road in advance of the convoy, and sow the area with mines (if available) to take out trucks and personnel. The convoy would draw to a halt, and as soon as the crews disembarked to clear the road the guerrillas would open up with heavy AK fire for short durations, just long enough to create casualties amongst the Soviet troops, before picking up any dropped Soviet weapons and disappearing back into the mountains. Like Vietnam, the AK proved itself to be an excellent ambush weapon, combining the requisite accuracy (through its controllability), killing power and rate of fire to cause hideous damage amongst concentrated troops.

Other AK-type weapons were used to good effect by the Mujahideen. The Dragunov SVD became a primary sniping tool of the guerrillas. Soviet forces tended to gather in huge camps on the outskirts of cities, as an act of intimidation over the local populace. The SVD has a range of 1300m (4265ft), and so Mujahideen snipers could fire occasional rounds from nearby mountains into the camps, killing Soviet officers and causing disarray and inefficiency within the Soviet logistics chain. During some convoy ambushes, Soviet RPK machine guns were also applied to enhance the firepower.

The Soviet occupation of Afghanistan lasted ten years, during which time the Soviets lost thousands of men to the weapons that their own Kalashnikov had invented or inspired. It is an apt illustration of how the AK has altered the balance of power between infantrymen on the battlefield, and how its distribution has increased the capability of informal fighting groups. The Soviets eventually left their occupation of Afghanistan, in no small part because of the steady deaths it received at the hands of its own weapons.

Kalashnikov's AK is undoubtedly a global weapon in distribution. Yet it is not possible to generalise about the AK or give it a neat label. The success of Kalashnikov's weapon has been the catalyst for a huge variety of imitations, variations and modifications. The following chapter will look across the world to see how various countries, as well as the former Soviet Union, have created entire series of weapons out of Kalashnikov's one initial design.

METHODS OF AK SMUGGLING (SOUTH AFRICA)

An AK and/or its ammunition are often transferred across the border concealed in boxes of food, particularly a loose, dry food such as rice.

Cross-border trains provide a particularly convenient mode of arms smuggling. AKs are either contained within luggage or sometimes hidden in compartments within the train's structure.

Trucks provide the most significant method of large scale illegal importation. The weapons are concealed in either the truck's load or in the vehicle's axle containers. For example, 15 AKs can be concealed in a fuel tank and even tyres are used to contain AK ammunition. The advantage of truck importation is that the weight of traffic over the border makes it almost impossible to police effectively.

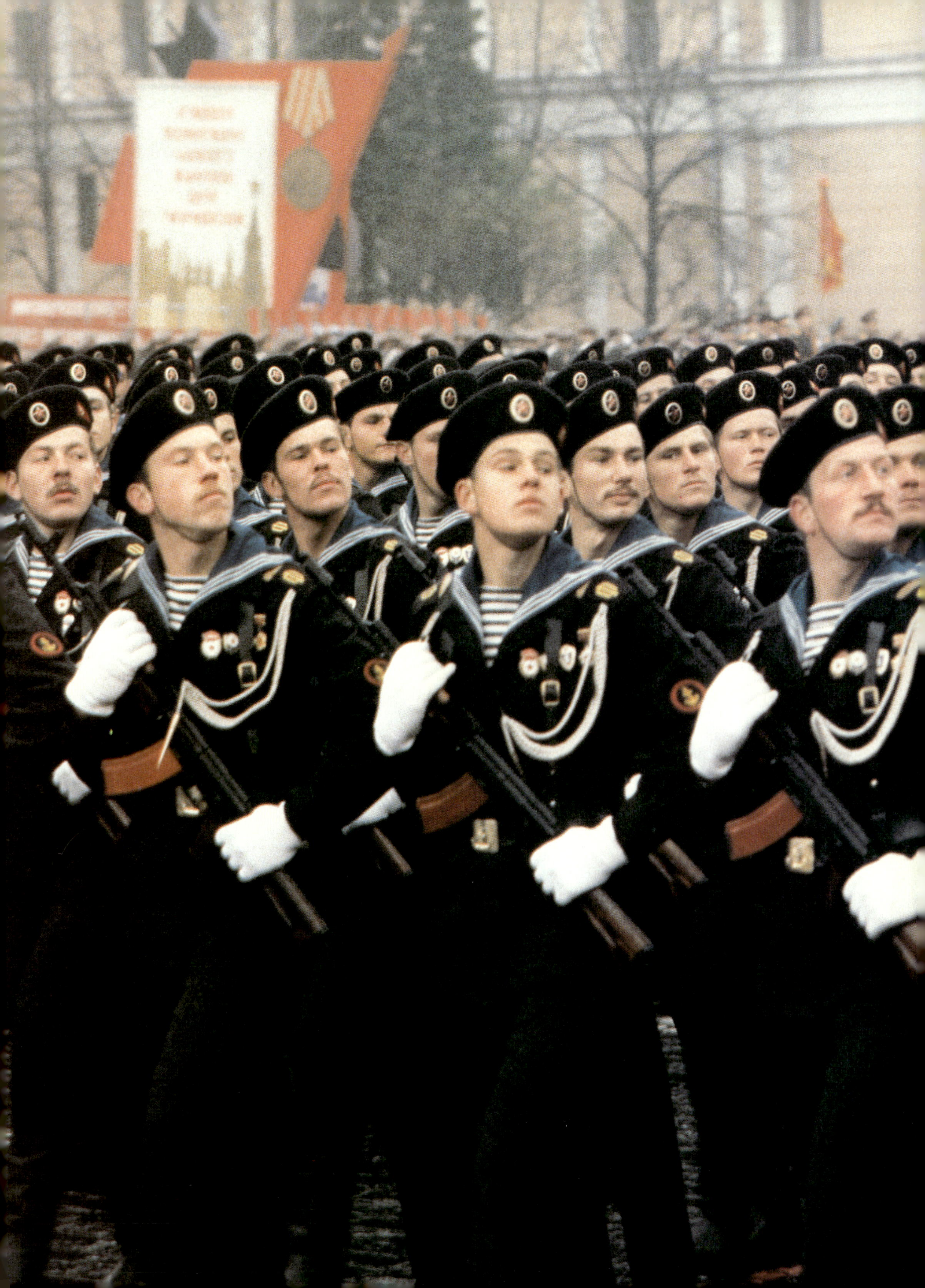

CHAPTER 5

AK Variants

The range of AK variants is truly bewildering. Once the AK47's qualities became recognised, an explosion of modification and transposition occurred, taking the basic assault rifle and turning it into a full-spectrum range of submachine guns, machine guns, other formats of rifle, shotguns and sniper rifles.

Nor is this process confined to the former Soviet Union. Licensed production agreements and outright imitation spread around the world. Variants appeared in huge numbers within every continent upon earth, in countries as diverse as China, Bulgaria and Cuba.

The fact that some 80 million AK-type rifles have spread around the world makes the study of variants an enormously complex subject to tackle. This chapter approaches this problem in two sections. Firstly, we will deal with the most fundamental variants of the AK produced within the Soviet Union and CIS. In particular here, we will closely follow the story of the AK74 – the 5.45mm development of the AKM – which has become the dominant successor to the standard 7.62mm rifle. From the AK74 we will then look at the broad sweep of Russian modifications, from the AK100 series of assault rifles to the RPK machine guns and the SVD sniper rifle.

Following our study of Russian variants, we will then do a country-by-country assessment of global variants. This will not only include licensed weapons produced within the Warsaw Pact, but also look at weapons which took the AK as their inspiration - the Israeli Galil and the Finnish Valmet being examples. By taking this extensive journey, we can complete our picture of the full influence of the AK47. For wherever there is a conflict in the world, AKs are usually present somewhere in the military mix.

THE AK74

In 1974 a new rifle appeared in the hands of Russian soldiers. It was recognisably an AK gun – the general configuration was basically the same as the AK47 – apart from a long

Left: Soviet naval infantry parade displaying the AK74 assault rifle. Though of a much smaller calibre than its 7.62mm parent, its lethality is actually greater because of ammunition design and high velocity.

Above: The AK74 is instantly recognisable in the hands of these Russian paratroopers. The long muzzle-brake/compensator gives it a slender appearance as well as a stunning accuracy.

eye-catching muzzle-brake fitting. Most importantly, however, was that this weapon was no longer using the now venerable 7.62 x 39mm M43. Instead, it fired a much smaller 5.45mm round at much higher velocities. This weapon was the AK74, and it signalled the AK rifle's coming of age in the modern world of small-arms development.

Like the AK47, the AK74 was born because of the production of a new type of ammunition. In the mid-1960s Soviet military analysts were being awoken to the performance advantages of small-calibre rounds, particularly once combat data began to feed back from the burgeoning conflict in Vietnam. Here the US forces had shifted from the heavy 7.62mm M14 rifle to the lighter 5.56mm M16A1 as its standard. Some of these weapons fell into Soviet hands and the testing began. The results of analysis were revealing and compelling. Perhaps most practically important was that the small-calibre round naturally produced less recoil, and this correlated with a potential reduction in training times for soldiers. This was valuable in the context of tight military budgets where long periods of marksmanship training were not feasible. Additionally, the added controllability of the small-calibre rifle provided an increased accuracy, this equating with a greater first-hit probability. Soldiers could also carry almost twice the amount of rounds for the same weight as the previous cartridge.

However, the advantages of the small-calibre round were not just related to user friendliness. They also had ballistic advantages. Small-calibre rounds had a high velocity for low weight (up to 1000mps/3280fps), and in flight the high velocity gave a better flat-trajectory distance. Penetration might not have been as good as some of the larger rounds, but lethality was just as good, if not better. Very high-velocity bullets impart a huge degree of hydrostatic shock – an effect in which the water content of body tissue effectively ripples from the supersonic air pressure, causing horrible damage.

All these factors combined to make the case for adopting the small-calibre round very persuasive. Development of a Soviet version began at the Russian arms manufacturer TsNIITochmash. Ammunition designers and technicians such as Viktor Sabelnikov and Lydia Boulavskaya originally arrived at a round designated the 13MZh. The calibre of the 13MZh was 5.6 x 39mm, but further design improvements led them to the 13MZhV – 5.45 x 39mm. The 13MZhV (which became known as the M74) had a 3.4gm (0.12oz) bullet, a 1.45gm (0.05oz) propellant charge (both of these measurements are out of a total weight of 10.2gm/0.36oz) and an overall length of 57mm (2.24in). Its muzzle velocity was an impressive 900mps (2953fps). What was needed was a weapon to fire it.

The answer was the AK74, today the standard infantry assault rifle of the CIS forces. Unlike the AK47 which was a competitive winner for the M43 round, the AK74 was developed in tandem with the M74 by two engineers surnamed Alexandrov and Nesterov. They initially accommodated the round in modified versions of the AK47 and AKM, the latter modification eventually becoming the AK74. Yet the AK74 should not be thought of as simply a recalibrated AKM. Many improvements were built into the AK74 by design or by consequence. Weight in the AK74 is 3.1kg (6.8lb) as opposed to the 3.85kg (8.4lb) of the AKM. The weight of the bolt was also reduced because of the smaller cartridge. The result of this was that the bolt carrier to bolt weight ratio increased: the AKM had a 5:1 ratio whereas the AK74 has a 6:1 ratio. These dry technical details hide the practical result that the proportionately heavier bolt carrier on the AK74 gave even better feed reliability, the bolt carrier being able to provide more secure bullet seating. The extractor mechanism was also improved to give better ejection. Ejection of the M74 case from the AK74 can be up to a distance of 6m (20ft). Whether such brisk ejection is necessary or even desirable is open to question, but the general feel is of a gun that is solid in both its operating system and its ejection.

The feature which separates the AK74 from its predecessors is its long, cylindrical muzzle brake. It will be remembered the AKM had a compensator, not a brake. By being cut at an angle the AKM's muzzle deflected some of the gas blast upwards to counteract muzzle climb, but not recoil. The AK74 is different. Its muzzle brake takes a sophisticated approach to controlling gas flow, directing jets in various directions to stop muzzle climb, reduce recoil and alleviate some of the sideways blast that many muzzle brakes produce which can impact on those stood next to the firer. The net result is a gun which only imparts 2.11ft/lbs of recoil force on the stock compared to the M16's 4.42ft/lbs and the AKM's 6.41ft/lbs. Full-auto 30-round bursts are thus quite possible with the AK74 while retaining accuracy, and this adds up to an increased killing potential for any trained soldier.

Apart from the muzzle brake, there are several other features which separate the AK74 from the AK47 and AKM and which act as key identifiers. The furniture on the first batches of AK74s was the same wood-laminated plastic as the AKM or resin-impregnated wood fibre. It soon changed to new all-polymer furniture which is lighter and very tough (AK74s can also be seen with red polymer magazines). Today's AK74s have the same style of furniture though the colour tends to be black or grey. In all cases, however, long grooves are cut into the stocks which identify them as 5.45mm calibre – a necessary precaution to a new or night-

Below: Soviet naval infantry charge during a training assault. The AK74 has a portability advantage over the AK47, weighing over 1kg (2.2lb) less than the original Kalashnikov.

time user to stop them attempting to fire 7.62mm rounds from the gun by mistake. In all modern cases grooves are cut into the top of the receiver to take optical sights.

The AK74 has continued the excellence of the AK47, and it has been popularly received by almost all. The Appendix gives some details of the weapon which may replace the AK74 – the AN-94 – but many are questioning whether the new, more sophisticated weapon will still have all the reliability and combat realism of the AK weapon. An updated version of the AK74, known as the AK74M (for 'modernised'), was produced in 1987 as a competitive challenge to the AN-94 in competitions held in Abakan. The most prominent improvement over the standard AK74 is a hinged stock which folds if required along the left of the receiver – a feature intended to replace the need for the fixed stock AK74 and its folding-stock version, the AKS74. It also featured strengthening at key points of the weapon, such as using wear resistant plastic for the furniture and making the muzzle-brake/compensator attachment more solid. Yet indications are that the gun has been overshadowed by the AN-94 and the AK74M fell out of production in 1992.

OTHER SOVIET/CIS VARIANTS

The AK74 is just the tip of the iceberg of AK variants within the former Soviet Union. Having brought ourselves up-to-date with the basic assault rifle, we will now move backwards and forwards through time to look at the breadth of weapons which have emerged since 1947 to take advantage of the AK's operating method and qualities. For convenience, it is easiest to separate these weapons into the major categories of assault rifles, submachine guns, machine guns and sniper rifles. (Note: being military in orientation this book will not cover the many civilian weapons derived from the AK. For a good source on this

Below: This AKS74 is fitted with a 40mm 6G15 underbarrel grenade launcher. Other fitments can include optical, infra-red and image-intensifying sights to give the weapon advanced combat capabilities.

Right: Weapons like the AK103 here pictured signal a return to the 7.62mm M43 calibre. Kalashnikovs of the 100 series are available in common calibres in an attempt to open new export markets.

see Val Shilin and Charlie Cutshaw, *Legends and Reality of the AK:* Paladin Press, 2000.)

ASSAULT RIFLES

The AK74 did not signal the end of AK assault rifle development in Russia. Recently there has emerged the AK-100 series of assault rifles and submachine guns, a series which provides the AK configuration in a full range of old and new calibres. Falling into the category of assault rifle are the AK-101, AK-103, AK-107 and AK-108. The AK-101 is essentially an AK74 but chambered for the US 5.56 x 45mm round. The recalibration is an export advantage: with the 5.56mm round in such widespread use around the world the AK-101 is able to access a broader diversity of markets (though the AK-101 keeps four-groove rifling rather than the six-grooves used by most other 5.56mm rifles). Using a different round changes the shape of the magazine, and the AK-101 can be recognised by a straighter magazine than the AK74.

Similarly, the AK-103 is a recalibrated AK74, this time returning to the 7.62mm calibre of the M43. Some modifications have been made to the gun's construction. The gas-port assembly has a square appearance which is quite distinctive and improvements have been made to the efficiency of the AK74 muzzle-brake/compensator. Like the AK74M, the butt is of the hinged variety and all the furniture features either chequered grip (pistol grip) or ribbed grip (fore-end) surfaces for better hand adhesion. Optical- or electro-optical sight rails are fitted to the left of the receiver.

Perhaps more distinctive than the AK-101 and AK-103 are the AK-107 and AK-108. The story of these two guns actually

Right: The Soviet soldier on the left – attending to the Armenian earthquake in 1989 – is carrying an AKS-74U submachine gun. This extremely compact weapon is much used by Russian special forces.

AK VARIANTS

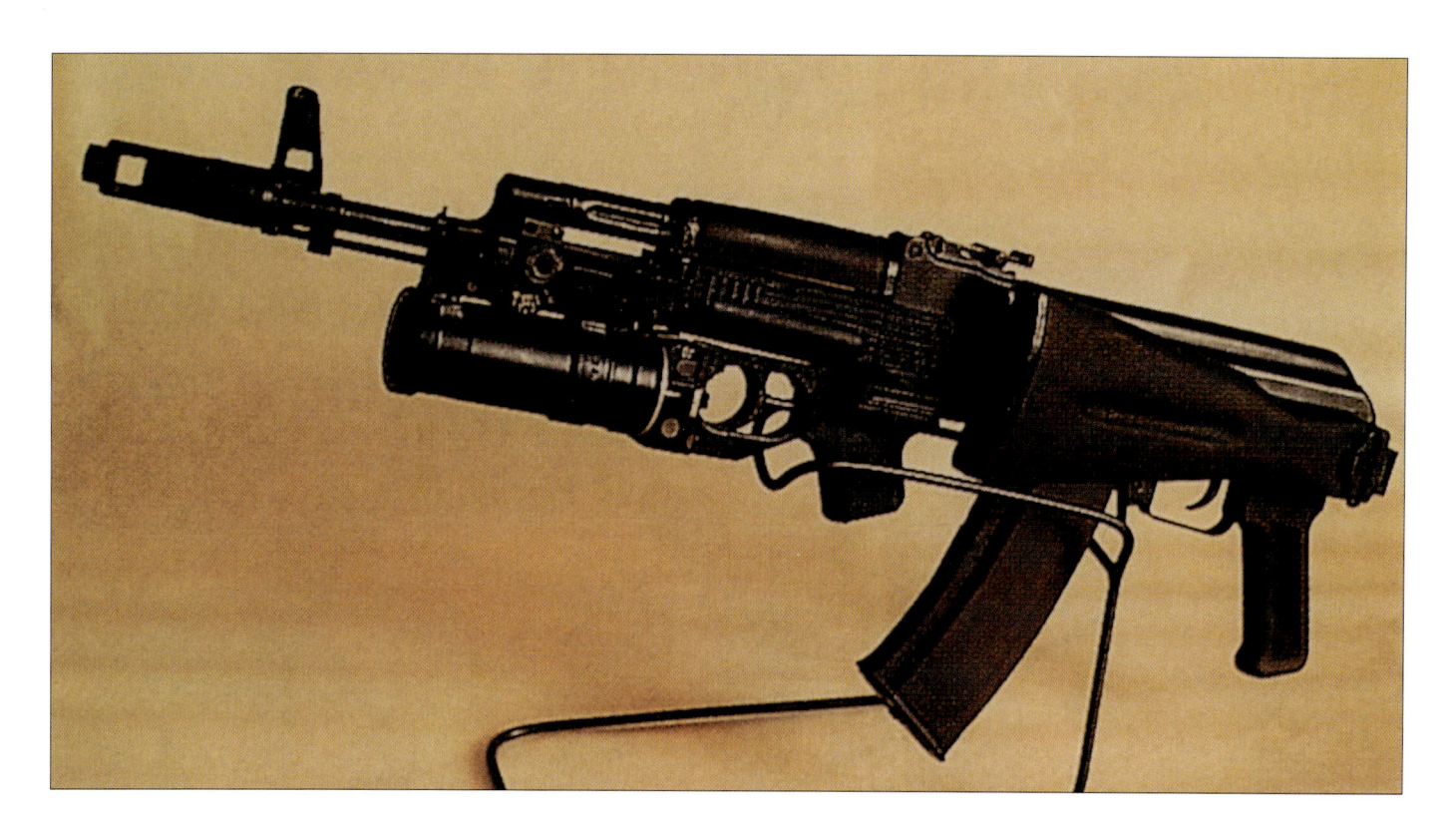

Above: Here the receiver cover of the AKS-74U is lifted to reveal the recoil spring. The dimensions of this weapon are extremely compact – with its stock folded it measures only 420mm (16.5in).

begins back at the time when a new gun was being sought for the M74 round. We now know that the AK74 took that role, but another, developed at the time, showed an ingenious act of engineering which has been resurrected in the AK-107 and AK-108.

This other weapon was the AL-7 designed by Yuri Alexandrov at Izhmash and completed in prototype in 1969. What was ingenious about the AL-7 was a system called 'balanced automatics' which was intended to entirely eliminate recoil. This it did by featuring a counter-recoil system which was propelled forward at the very moment the bolt carrier was driven back upon firing. The two parts were synchronised so that the forces reached their maximum travel and their closed positions at exactly the same moment – this enabled the exact counteraction of the recoil forces and resulted in a gun which scarcely moved at all upon firing.

The AK74 won out over the AL-7 because the latter was far more expensive to produce for the time. Now, however, the AL-7 has been recreated in the AK-107/108, in fact there is little between the guns except a three-round burst facility in the later weapons. The reasons for revisiting this design are a lack of commercial success from the other AK-100 guns and the extreme cheapness of AK47s and AKMs leading to the need for more profit-making weapon lines. The AK-107 and -108 are meant to be of greater interest to more developed Western and Far Eastern markets that can invest in quality weaponry. The AK-107 comes in 5.45 x 39mm calibre while the AK-108 is a 5.56 x 45mm weapon, both rifles acting to cover all potential markets. We have yet to see how the sales of this weapon proceed, but the performance of the rifle is undoubtedly good with a high rate of fire (850–900rpm) balanced by an accuracy estimated at 1.5 times that of the AK74.

The principles of the AL-7 found further Kalashnikov application in the AKB and AKB-1 assault rifles. These were designed by the Kalashnikov Design Bureau for the Abakan weapon selection programme in the late 1980s early 1990s (of which the AN-94 was the winner as the new standard assault rifle). The AKB-1 actually came first in 1985 and utilised balanced automatics. Yet this time the forward-moving element was the barrel itself. An improved version, the AKB, was produced and showed many sophisticated features. These included burst mode – the first two rounds of automatic fire have a greatly increased cyclical rate, 2000rpm, before returning to its more 'normal' 1000rpm (excessively high for an assault rifle). The details of the Akaban Project are difficult to come by, but we now know that the AKB was beaten by Nikonov's AN-94. What is clear is that the Kalashnikov Bureau are straying away from the

Above: The Czech-manufactured LADA assualt rifle, first seen in 1993. The weapon has two possible rounds, the Eastern Bloc 5.45 x 39mm or the NATO 5.56 x 45mm.

simplicity of Kalashnikov's original spirit, and it is unclear whether this will actually aid the soldier on the battlefield in any meaningful way.

SUBMACHINE GUNS

Soviet investment in submachine design fell to an all-time low in the early post-war period once the rationale behind assault rifles took hold. Yet during the 1960s counter-terrorism and counter-insurgency achieved a vogue in military thinking and required the compact, potent firepower offered by submachine guns. (Many other countries were producing ultra-small submachine guns – the Uzi, Skorpion, Ingram Mac 10 etc – so the USSR also wanted to keep up.) This process has been given a further boost in Russia's post-communist era which has been stricken with violent organised crime. In this climate submachine guns have once again become preferred tools of the special police units, giving hard take-down power but reducing the risk of civilian deaths and injuries through over-penetration of rounds.

Almost all the major AK rifles now have carbine versions. The initial rationale behind such developments was to provide various specialist troops with compact weapons compatible with standard forms of AK ammunition and magazines. Those to receive such weapons included Spetsnaz forces, tank, truck, APC and rocket-launcher crews, engineers, airborne forces, and police units. In the standard 7.62 x 39mm M43 a shortened variant of the AKM, the AKMS-U, was produced after winning a competition to find a weapon that could be easily fired from vehicle ports. Its overall length, even with the butt extended, is only 722mm (28.4in) and its rate of fire is high – about 800rpm – owing to the standard hammer-delay mechanism of the AKM being omitted. With a barrel length of only 225mm (8.8in) sighting expectations show more of a realism than the standard assault rifle. The back 'L' sight can be adjusted for ranges of between 100–500m (328–1640ft), and the point of impact can also be altered by twisting the front site. Today, the AK-104 provides the 7.62mm submachine gun variant. To all intents and purposes this is a shortened AK-103, its butt-folded length taken down to 586mm (23in). Like many AK submachine guns, the AK-104 features a distinctive conical flash hider – an essential feature to reduce the prodigious muzzle flash that results from firing the rifle rounds from such shortened barrels. The AK-104 is easily distinguished if the AK-103 rifle is familiar, but there are slight differences such as a lack of cleaning rod beneath the barrel and a lack of bayonet lug (such features can catch on clothes and equipment in confined spaces).

The introduction of the 5.45 x 39mm round in the early 1970s detracted attention away from submachine design for some time, with the AK74 drawing the focus of weapons design to the assault rifle. Yet before long the new calibre required its own submachine gun variants. Two main types are in production. The first was the natural derivative of the AK74, the shortened AKS-74U. This stocky gun has a length of only 420mm (16.53in), and both barrel and gas tube are radically shortened to achieve these dimensions. As always with carbines, the challenge is to design the gun so that it can cope with the increased forces of both gas-piston operation and recoil. In the AKSU-74 this is achieved through an expansion chamber fitted to the muzzle which reduces the pressure levels going into the gas-piston mechanism. Further alterations from the standard AK74 include a front-hinged receiver cover. The AKS-U74 was also produced in two sub-variants, the AKS-74UN and the AKS-74Y. The former of these weapons is the standard carbine adapted to take a passive infra-red sight, while the latter has an integral silencer fitted for special operation forces.

In 1997, the AKS-U74 was taken out of production. The 5.45mm submachine gun has been continued, like many of the Kalashnikov weapons, in the AK-100 series. This variant is designated the AK-105, and is the 5.45mm version of the AK-104, with no other distinguishing features apart from the straighter magazine that accompanies the 5.45mm round. Though the other 5.45mm weapon in the AK-100 series, the AK-107, has an advanced cyclic rate of fire of 850+ rpm, the AK-105 keeps the restraint of the AK-104 with an average 600rpm.

Finally in the AK range of submachine guns is the AK-102 in 5.56 x 45mm. Like the other shortened weapons in the AK-100 series, this is simply a scaled-down version of its rifle counterpart, in this case the AK-101. The magazine is yet

Below: The RPK74 is the 5.45mm squad-automatic version of the standard AK74 assault rifle. It fires from 30-, 40- or 45-round box magazines with a cyclic rate of fire of 850rpm.

straighter than even the 5.45mm versions, thus providing a visual identifier. Despite the gun's practical range of about 300m (984ft), there is the facility to take optical and electro-optical sights via a rail on the left side of the receiver. Shared with the submachine-gun family in the AK-100 series is the bulbous gas-expansion chamber and muzzle-brake unit.

Before moving on to machine guns and sniper rifles, one more submachine gun is worth noting for its distinctive relationship with the AK family. The Bizon is a true submachine gun (the weapons above stray more towards the carbine category), in that it actually fires a pistol-calibre round. Its calibre is 9mm, but it has the versatile option of taking almost any standard 9mm round, the magazine being able to adapt to various pistol cartridge lengths without special modification.

Its significance in our AK story is two-fold. Firstly, it was designed in 1994 by none other than Viktor Kalashnikov, the son of Mikhail Timofeyevich, and the son of another great arms designer, Alexey Dragunov. This pairing had produced early submachine guns in tandem, such as the PP-71M and Klin-2. But these weapons were independent designs from the AK series, whereas the Bizon shares some 60 per cent parts with the AK74M, including an identical trigger mechanism. Despite having a much cruder appearance than most of the AK rifles, the Bizon is recognisable as a Kalashnikov. Its muzzle, front sight, selector switch and receiver cover are all AK parts. The stock is a simple metal frame hinged to fold along the left side of the receiver. The Bizon has been produced in three variations, each offering subtle improvements in either sighting or furniture. All, however, give a respectable performance. Firing from a 65-round magazine, the gun will put out a cyclical 650rpm burst with good stability and a fearsome knock-down power over a range of 100m (328ft). Unlike the AK rifles, the Bizon works on the simple blow-back mechanism common to most true submachine-gun types (i.e. weapons which fire a pistol round), yet

Above: The Polish Radom-Hunter 7.62 x 39mm semi-automatic sniper rifle. The soundness of the Kalashnikov design has led to many fine sniper rifles, though the parts and barrels are machined to much higher tolerances.

it offers many of the positive qualities of reliability provided by the Kalashnikov weapons proper. In today's crime-ridden CIS, the Bizon is proving to be a popular weapon amongst special police and anti-terrorism units on the streets of the Russia's cities.

MACHINE GUNS

The concept of the light machine had gained currency during World War I. During the muddy assaults on the Western Front, both sides realised that there would be tremendous advantage in having a machine gun that would be light enough to be carried by one man, and which was capable of being quickly set up to provide supporting firepower in seconds. This brief would be fulfilled in various weapons over the next three decades, reaching from almost useless weapons such as the French Fusil Mitrailleur M'15 Chauchat to commanding firearms like the British Bren gun.

Although the light machine gun reached superlative levels of engineering in World War II, the post-war world saw a significant development of the form to make it even more practically integrated in troop manoeuvres. During World War II, guns such as the German MG42 had demonstrated what has been termed the 'modular approach'. This meant that such weapons could be used in both heavy and light fire roles depending on the type of mounting but still utilising the same type of ammunition as standard rifles. The modular approach had several advantages, not least that should the machine gun run out of ammunition, resupply could usually be gleaned from rifle stocks. History has now shown the dual-purpose machine gun to be an excellent concept. German troops armed with an MG42, for example, could one minute be supporting an assault with devastating firepower from close ranges, then have the gun tripod-mounted for potent low-level anti-aircraft fire the next.

In the post-war environment, the focus shifted slightly. As reduced-power rounds became dominant in both Eastern and Western Bloc armies, it became apparent that modularism could be taken a stage further. The step taken was to use the standard assault rifle as the physical basis for the light machine gun itself, utilising the same magazines for battlefield convenience and simply using a heavier and longer barrel, bipod-supported to extend the range and accuracy. The concept today is labelled the 'Light Support Weapon' or 'Squad Automatic Weapon', and the Kalashnikov weapons were some of the first in the world to receive such treatment.

In the 1960s the Soviet military authorities were looking for a replacement for the belt-fed RPD machine gun. Kalashnikov provided the answer. From 1961 the new SAW was the Ruchnoi Pulemet Kalashnikova (RPK). Its calibre was the same as the AKM, and indeed it could take the AKM or AK47 magazines as standard, though typically it used 40-round boxes or 75-round drums to better enhance its support role. Yet the operator had to show caution in his firing technique. Like many SAWs even today, the RPK had no barrel-change facility like light machine guns. This meant that overheating could be a real problem with sustained firing – the barrel could become super-hot and start spontaneously firing rounds in the chamber. As Ezell has also pointed out, the fact that the RPK also fired from a closed-bolt made the problem worse, as open-bolt weapons help the through-flow of air down the barrel to assist cooling.

Yet the RPK was still a sound weapon, mainly because it was almost identical to the AK rifle in mechanism and construction. The only differences were a longer (590mm/23.22in) barrel, bipod-supported, a strengthened receiver, and a rear sight capable of windage adjustment. It also had a deep stock with an entirely different shape, 'deep bellied' to give the left hand a grip surface during firing from the prone position. One problem with the RPK, however, was that the bottom-loading configuration meant that the 40-round magazine necessitated a rather tall bipod, thus giving the user problems in maintaining a low level of cover and also in depressinging the muzzle below the horizontal from a prone position. Muzzle velocity on the RPK is 732mps (2400fps), only 30mps (98fps) different from the AK rifle, but ranges of 800m (2624ft) could be sustained in reality because of the barrel length. A variant of the RPK, the RPKS, was produced to meet the needs of special forces and armoured troops which featured a folding butt for more convenient storage and carriage.

The Kalashnikov design lived on in another series of 7.62mm weapons, the PK family. In essence, however, the PK guns are not Kalashnikov's and cannot be externally recognised as such. The Kalashnikov input to the PK family was the excellent rotating bolt, with the other elements of the weapons borrowed from existing firearms. More strictly part of the Kalashnikov family is the RPK74. As its name instantly suggests, this is the SAW version of the AK74. As the RPK is to the AKM, so the RPK74 is to the AK74, with a longer and heavier barrel than the standard rifle and a bipod fitting. The barrel length and grooving are the same as the RPK, but the muzzle velocity is much higher – about 925mps (3034fps) – in line with the high-velocity ammunition. Ammunition feed is from 30-, 40- or 45-round magazines, and the narrower case gives a length shortening advantage over the tall RPK magazines. Several variations have also been produced. The RPKS-74 has a folding butt and the RPKS-74N is fitted with a night sight.

The RPK74 was not the final word in Kalashnikov light-machine gun development. In the mid to late 1970s, Mikhail Dragunov and Viktor Kalashnikov once more formed a team. This time their project was the design of a new light machine gun which would not only be fed from the standard AK- and RPK-74 magazines, but which could also use 150-, 200- or 250-round belts for sustained-fire roles. The result was the PU series of firearms. This series consisted of three main types: the PU-1, PU-2 and PU-21. The PU-1 was basically the RPK74 with a belt-feed mechanism fitted – belts are fed in from the left – and interestingly enough it retained the single-shot function of the AK74 rifle. This selective-fire mode was dropped in the PU-2 and PU-21, and using the Goryunov belt-feed mechanism of the PK weapons these two weapons

RPK

AK VARIANTS

could accept belt feed from either side (magazine feed was restricted to the left on all three models). Both the PU-2 and the PU-21 retained Kalashnikov elements in various parts, but by the time the gun was ready to go into production they shared few features with existing Soviet ranges of firearms. This counted severely against them, and so the PU family were consigned to the drawing board and prototype models without ever entering service.

SNIPER RIFLES

Most works on the AK47 include the Dragunov SVD sniper rifle as part of the AK extended family. The inclusion, however, can be questioned. Admittedly, the SVD is built around the standard AK gas-action, something which is visibly noticeable in the design of the weapon. However, the SVD has three locking lugs instead of two on the bolt. Build onto this fact that it was designed by Evgeny Dragunov and Ivan Samoylov, actually defeating Kalashnikov designs in the competitive trials of the late 1950s, plus the use of the old 7.62 x

Left: A NATO soldier on exercise in Poland stops to check his AK rifle. Note the 40mm grenade launcher beneath the barrel. Grenade launchers are becoming a much more commonplace fitment on modern AKs.

Calibre:	7.62 x 39mm M43
Length:	1041mm (41in)
Weight:	4.76kg (10.5lb)
Feed:	30- or 40-round detachable box magazine, or 75-round drum
System of operation:	Gas-operated, rotating bolt
Rate of fire (cyclic):	600rpm
Muzzle velocity:	732mps (2400fps)

Left: Here UNITA soldiers in southern Angola are armed with Chinese Type 56 assault rifles. China recently built an AK ammunition factory in Africa.

54R calibre, and it seems odd that the SVD is included in the Kalashnikov family.

Yet the Kalashnikov gas-operation does secure some family possession over the SVD, if only for the sake of interest. The SVD is unusual in that most precision sniper rifles are bolt action, whereas the SVD is a semi-automatic, magazine-fed weapon. Self-loading weapons are generally avoided in sniping because it is felt that the abuse the cartridge undergoes in the loading process affects the bullet's accuracy. Such is true, but for functional use up to around 1000m (3280ft) the Dragunov has proved itself in combat as a thoroughly proficient weapon (see Chapter 4).

The SVD is a long, slender weapon – 1220mm (48.03in) long with a barrel length of 545mm (21.45in) It is easily identified by its exposed barrel and its cutaway butt/pistol grip, along with a general similarity to the AK rifles. The SVD fires the old rimmed 7.6254R cartridge to lend it its range, though the magazine requires ribs running up the side to guide the rimmed round into its proper seating. It is usually sighted through the PSO-1 424 optical sight, this giving it a maximum range of up to 1300m (4265ft) and an excellent first-round hit probability at distances of up to 800m (2624ft). Mounting brackets are fitted to the left side of the receiver.

The SVD has seen a great deal of combat action in its lifespan, and it has proved itself a capable sniping tool despite its self-loading function (or more likely because of this function). Its convincing performance has meant that Russia maintains production of the guns to this day. Sights have naturally been upgraded. The standard optical sight is the 424 PSO-1M2 while the SVDN2 uses the NSPUM electro-optical sight and the SVDN3 the NSPU-3 large-body sight for work at shorter distances. Such weapons are likely to be seen in active service for many decades to come.

Thus ends the general run of Soviet/Russian/CIS AK variations. There are several weapons on which we have not had the space to focus, particularly the civilian weapons such as the Sayga shotguns. Yet we can now see that the basic Kalashnikov operating system has an incredible appeal for weapons designers. By using it they instantly gain purchase on reliability and consistency, and as we turn our eyes to look at the rest of the world this lesson in borne up time and time again.

For reasons of space, our run though the world-wide variants of the AK47 will be necessarily brief. For more information on the numbers of AK weapons deployed or made around the world, see Chapter 4. However, here we will take a country-by-country overview of those who have produced variants of the AK within their borders, either through licensed production or through imitation.

ARMENIA

The only AK variant to be produced in Armenia is the distinctive 5.45mm Model 3 assault rifle. It actually follows a 'bullpup' configuration – that is, the magazine is situated behind the pistol-grip. The effect of this layout is to reduce the overall length of the gun (the Model 3 is 700mm/27.6in) while being able to retain a useful barrel length (415mm/16.3in). Thus most of the firing qualities are the exact match of the AK74. The Model 3 can take optical or electro-optical sights on the left side of the receiver, and its furniture is of a distinctive dark-green plastic. The Model 3 was brought into service in 1996.

Left: FLE soldiers in Eritrea launch an attack on Ethiopian positions with their AKs. The AK is so simple to use that even the most poorly trained soldier will be able to create and control serious firepower.

Dragunov SVD

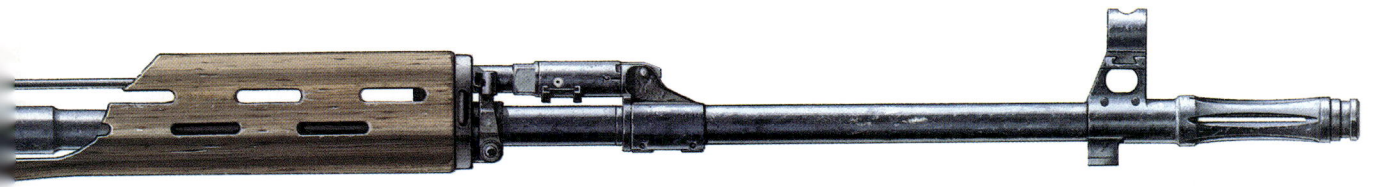

Calibre:	7.62 x 54R Soviet
Length:	1225mm (48.2in)
Weight:	4.31kg (9.5lb)
Feed:	10-round detachable box magazine
System of operation:	Gas-operated, rotating bolt
Rate of fire (cyclic):	N/A
Muzzle velocity:	828mps (2720fps)

BULGARIA

Post-war Bulgaria has relied almost entirely on Eastern Bloc weapons provision. Up until the mid-1960s, these weapons mainly came through Polish supply (either as whole weapons or later as parts to be assembled). However, by the mid-1960s its own licensed production began, this giving rise to three fundamental models which tracked the development of the Soviet AK. The first of these, produced in the state arsenals, was the AKK. This is almost identical in every way to the AK47, though receiver markings are different and the selector markings which have 'ЕД' instead of the 'ОД' as on the Russian guns. Next to follow was the AKKM assault rifle in the 1970s, again almost identical apart from markings to the AKM weapon. Finally, the mid-1980s saw the appearance of the AKK-74, naturally related to the AK74 and bearing the same points of distinction as the guns already listed. With each successive variation, a folding butt variety has also been produced, these being listed like the Russian/Soviet weapons with an 'S' in their title.

PEOPLE'S REPUBLIC OF CHINA

The close ideological liaison between the Soviet Union and China during the Cold War led to the USSR assisting in the establishment of weapon production facilities within China. Thus by the mid-1950s China was producing both SKS and AK assault rifles, and would go on to be one of the largest external producers of such firearms. The fundamental model which serves the country to this day is the Type 56. To all intents and purposes, this is straight AK47 copy, the only distinguishing features being the Chinese selector markings and markings such as the number 66 placed in a triangle – this indicates that the gun was manufactured in State Factory No 66. Production methods of the Type 56 closely followed Soviet lines. As with the AK47, the Type 56 receiver was initially constructed from a single machined block of steel, but the mid-1960s saw a switch to steel pressing in sympathy with the AKM.

From the basic Type 56 came four main sub-variations, the changes usually revolving around the furniture configurations. The Type 56-1 featured a U-shaped folding steel butt in AKS47 pattern. Some care is needed in identification as the same designation is applied to the AKM style gun with a folding butt, and it should be noted that many of the 56-1s have no bayonet fitting. Following the Type 56-1 is the Type 56-2. This gun appeared in Chinese hands during the mid-1970s. Its butt is again the main focus for alteration – in this case the skeleton metal stock folds down along the side of the receiver. The butt also features a distinctive red-brown plastic cheek-piece to aid target shooting.

Below: The opening of relations between East and West since the Cold War has meant a much less protective interchange of ideas about small arms design. Here a US soldier gets acquainted with the AK.

AK VARIANTS

Bringing the 7.62mm sub-variants up to date are the Type 56-S and the Type 56-C. The first of these weapons was a semi-auto only version of the Type 56-2, a commercial model destined for the expanding market for AK-type weapons in the US. The latter gun was a shortened version of the Type 56, the overall dimensions taken down from 645mm (25.4in), butt folded length in the Type 56-1 to a compact 563mm (22.2in) and with minor variations in muzzle brake and sights.

Like the rest of the world, the 1970s and 1980s saw China moving to the small-calibre high-velocity round in its firearms. Thus the Type 56 became the Type 81 in 5.4545mm calibre in the basic format of the AK74 but with a fixed stock. The Type 81 was also issued in 5.5645mm in 1982, thus giving China the ability to access most markets with its weapons. Along with small-calibre rounds, another modern development in AK variations was the Type 86, an experimentation in 'bullpup' design. John Walter (in *Kalashnikov - machine pistols, assault rifles and machine guns, 1945 to the present:* Greenhill 1999) indicates that this weapon may have also been made in 5.45mm and 7.62mm, but as the rifle does not seem to have entered into production it is hard to know the truth of its circumstances.

EGYPT

Egypt's anti-Israel posture naturally aligned it with the Soviet Union, and it received large amounts of Eastern Bloc AK47s and AKMs. Furthermore, it also manufactured its own version of the AKM with Soviet assistance from the late 1960s. Named the Misr, it has few defining features in relation to the AKM, apart from Arabic markings. The Misr has been produced in fairly large quantities, and even a US version has been made in semi-automatic mode only with a ten-round magazine.

FINLAND

Finland's relationship with the Kalashnikov guns has been a particularly intensive one, with production levels reaching up to those of Warsaw Pact countries during the Cold War. Following the acquisition of Type III Kalashnikovs in 1950, titled in Finland as Ryannakkokiväari Malli 54 (M54), there followed some experimentation at the Valmet/Tourula arms factory which led to the M60 assault rifle. This was effectively an AK47 copy with furniture modifications – a tubular fixed butt – one of the Valmet's signatures, a fore-end of plastic-covered steel, and a repositioned rear sight at the back of the receiver with the front sight set back from the muzzle.

After a series of field trials an improved gun, the M62, was produced. This became the first major production model and was manufactured by Sako-Valmet AB. It was a solid

Right: A private of the Biafran army in east Nigeria, 1968, looks guarded with his AK47. Ammunition is stored in the bulky pouch worn on the left hip.

Above: A Kuwaiti soldier during the Gulf War squats and observes with an unloaded AK rifle. Like many Middle Eastern conflicts, the Gulf War made AKs face one another in combat.

performer, manufactured from steel pressings and using the plastic furniture and sight positioning used on the original AKM. The M62 was a reliable and effective gun like its inspiration, and there began a whole series of Valmet or Sako guns reaching up to the latest weapon, the M95. This series covers the three major world calibres – 5.56mm, 7.62mm and 5.45mm – and has proved to be excellent weaponry. Distinctive models include the heavy-barrelled M78 light machine gun and the M90 assault rifle with a transparent plastic magazine.

GERMAN DEMOCRATIC REPUBLIC

It is estimated that up to two million AK-type weapons were produced in East Germany. The East German variants began with the MPi-K assault rifle – a standard AK copy but without the butt trap of the Soviet weapons. German markings include 'D' above 'E' on the selector switches. The MPi-K was followed by a succession of modified versions, usually adaptations of the furniture material and buttstock. The MPi-KM had an unusual plastic stock with a grip texture of raised bumps, whereas the MPi-KMS and MPi-KMS72 featured side-folding rod-type butts. The MPi-K weapons were 7.6239mm in keeping with the Soviet weapons, and in 1983 a 5.45mm copy of the AK74 was produced in minor numbers. German reunification limited the production of this final weapon.

HUNGARY

Hungary has had a long relationship with the Kalashnikov, producing its own version of the AKM from the early 1960s. This was the AK-55, a copy of the AKM but demonstrating high standards of production in both furniture and metalworking, something not always found in Warsaw Pact production. The AK-55 was quickly improved, however, and became the AKM-63 in 1963. This had several features which set it apart from the Soviet inspiration. First, the fore-end was made integrally with the receiver out of sheet metal, something which gave very favourable production times and costs. It also had a pistol-grip fitted just ahead of the magazine for an alternative assault handling.

The AKM-63 spawned a light machine gun version, the AMD-65. This was a shortened version of the assault rifle. Butt-folded length reached to 598mm (23.54in), while its barrel was only 318mm (12.5in) with a 60mm (2.3in) muzzle compensator/flash hider. With its tubular folding butt which incorporates a shock absorber and a reciprocating forestock, the AMD-65 was intended for use by airborne

Right: USMC troops inspect captured Iraqi ordnance, which includes an RPG launcher and a Tabuk assault rifle. The Tabuk was Iraq's own version of the AKM and is difficult to identify from the AKM.

AK VARIANTS

Above: Polish reconnaissance troops ford a river, fronted by a soldier with an RPK squad automatic. Poland has made many of its own AK variants but so far has not produced an RPK imitation.

troops, and it could also take optical sights and grenade-launcher fittings.

All the above weapons fitted into the 7.62mm category. Outside of that specification fell the NGM assault weapons. The NGM-881 began its production life in 1981. Based on the AK74, it was in the M74's 5.45mm calibre and had few distinguishing features from the Soviet gun. Yet it was soon taken out of production in preference for making a 5.5645mm version, the NGM, which had more export currency than the Soviet version. The NGM subsequently went on to export markets in the US and various other countries.

IRAQ

Iraq's contribution to the AK family is the Tabuk assault rifle and Al Quds light machine gun. Both are almost identical copies of the AKM and RPK respectively, only distinguished by Arabic markings and slightly different butt shapes. Both guns were made in the standard M43 calibre, yet there is some suggestion that a 5.56mm variant of the rifle has also been made.

ISRAEL

Unlike Iraq, Israel has made some of the most original versions of the AK rifles. The standard Israeli weapon is the ARM (Galil). This was produced in 1967 as a replacement for the FN FAL rifle and utilised Israeli experience of confronting the AK47s and AKMs during the Six-Day War. Israeli designers decided that the AK operating system could not be bettered, and so produced what would go on be an excellent assault weapon. The ARM's derivation from the AK is clear, particularly at the receiver end (Finnish M62 Valmet receivers were used in initial production). The fore-end and barrel configuration, however, make a departure from the AK layout, with sights set back from the muzzle, a more boxy fluted fore-end (first of wood, then of nylon), an integral carrying handle, and distinctive fittings such as a standard bipod and a short flash hider/muzzle compensator. The butt is of the tubular type, this folding down alongside the right side of the receiver.

The Galil was an excellent design which serves the Israeli forces well to this day. 5.56mm chambering is the norm in Israel itself, but it has also produced the Galil in 7.62 x

Right: Syrian artillerymen rush to their positions during the Gulf War, AKs strapped to their backs. These weapons feature folding stocks, a configuration often preferred by artillery, vehicle and airborne crews.

Above: Romania's 7.62mm AIM assault rifle is distinctive on account of the integral pistol grip on the fore-end. When gripped by this the AIM has much more of a submachine gun style of fire.

51mm for export. Both versions come in the SAR version, simply a shortened carbine weapon, and the AR – little different from the ARM but lacking the bipod and carrying handle. Also of note is the Galil sniper rifle. Semi-automatic sniper rifles are not common, but the Galil sniper handles the format very successfully. It is essentially a standard Galil, but with a heavier barrel, a folding nylon butt featuring cheek rest and recoil pad, a fitting for an optical or electro-optical sight, and a generally heavier construction. A silencer can also be fitted, though only for use with special subsonic ammunition.

PEOPLE'S REPUBLIC OF KOREA

The Korean AKs are perhaps the poor relation of all the variants. AK-type weapons first fell into Korean hands when they started to receive consignments of Chinese Type 56 weapons in the 1960s. Yet they eventually decided to produce their own weapon series. The first off the production line was the Type 58 assault rifle, an AK47 copy but one which left a lot

THE AK47

Calibre:	5.56mm NATO
Length:	979mm (38.54in) stock extended; 742mm (29.21in) stock folded
Weight:	4.35kg (9.59lb)
Feed:	30- or 50-round detachable box magazine
System of operation:	Gas-operated
Rate of fire (cyclic):	650rpm
Muzzle velocity:	800mps (2624fps)

to be desired in the quality of production. This was superseded by an AKM version known as the Type 68. In both cases the quality was questionable, and these guns are often only identifiable through their Korean selector markings.

What the North Koreans lacked in quality they made up for in quantity. It is possible that some three million Type 58 and Type 68 rifles have been made, and the quantity is reflected in the fact that Korean weapons have now started to feature much more heavily in the international arms trade, both legal and illegal.

POLAND

To date Poland has produced up to 2.5 million AK-type rifles, making them one of the biggest producers outside of the former Soviet Union. The standard weapon is the 7.62mm PMK. Basically this is an AK47 copy, the different patterning on the pistol-grip being the only main sign of its individuality. From the PMK has come more distinctive variants. The PMK-DGN is a special grenade-launching version. This was designed to fire F1/N60 anti-personnel grenades and PGN-60 anti-tank grenades, the launching accomplished through a LON-1 unit (20mm) and the firer protected by a special recoil shoe.

Following the route of the Soviet weapons, the PMK yielded a folding stock version – the PMK-S – and later the AKM version known as the PMK-M (folding stock version, PMK-MS). As a more modern development, Poland has also produced a range of AK-type assault rifles and submachine guns in both 5.56 x 45mm and 5.45 x 39mm calibres. In the latter category falls the KA-88 Tantal assault rifle and the KA-89 Onyx submachine gun. The Tantal is a version of the AK-74S. Unlike the AK, however, it has the modern three-round burst facility and an ambidextrous selector operation. It also has a full range of accessories – sighting options include optical and electro-optical sights, plus laser range designators and a bolt-action 40mm Pallad grenade launcher.

The Onyx submachine is part of a substantial range of squat, powerful submachine-gun types produced by Poland on the AK pattern. It is little more than a shortened version of the KA-88 Tantal, and retains many of that gun's features. The Onyx has been updated in the KA-91 version, actually itself a short-barrelled version of the updated KA-90 Tantal assault rifle in 5.56mm calibre. Completing the 5.56mm range of Polish AKs, is the KA-96 Beryl assault rifle and its submachine-gun variant, the KbkA-96 Mini-Beryl. The Beryl assault rifle has a folding butt and rubber butt pad, offers the full range of fire selection modes, and can take a wide range of accessories like the KA-88 to enhance its combat performance. The Mini-Beryl, as its name suggests, is defined by

Galil ARM

compact dimensions – only 525mm (20.66in) with butt folded. Its barrel is a mere 235mm (9.25in), this bringing the muzzle-brake/flash-suppressor right up to the fore-end, though the gun still has fittings for various sighting devices.

Poland remains a productive source of AK-type weapons but has never been a total slave to the Soviet or Russian designs. It is interesting to speculate how the introduction of the AN-94 will affect its outlook.

ROMANIA

Romania has had a long-standing history of AK production, despite its small size and economic force. Three main versions form its 7.62mm calibre range. The AI assault rifle is a direct AK47 copy, with little but its selector markings (S - FA - FF) to define it. However, the Romanian version of the AKM, the AIM, started to show more originality. The key identifier to this weapon is the integral fore-end pistol grip, a feature which has run through most subsequent Romanian AK patterns. The exception to this rule is the AIR, the shortened version of the AIM. This omits the fore-end grip as standard, but having said that it can be fitted as an optional extra if required.

By the early 1980s the Romanians had diversified. They had produced their own version of the RPK light machine gun, and also taken the AIM rifle into a long sniper version, the FPK. Like the Soviet SVD, this used the 7.62 x 54R cartridge, and indeed the rifle is very similar in appearance to

KALASHNIKOV-TYPE SHOTGUNS

The Kalashnikov design has not only proven itself in assault rifles, but also in a range of commercial shotguns. Known as the Sayga series, the first of these was the Sayga-410. This appeared in 1994 and its receiver instantly identifies it as an AK derivative. In fact it is an AK rifle simply modified to a smooth-bore barrel calibrated to .410 cartridges. The feed is from a 2-, 4-, or 20-round detachable box magazine and the gun only shoots in semi-automatic mode. The Sayga 410 is one of a long line of Sayga shotguns, with 12-bore and 20-bore weapons also being available as well as the various other .410 weapons. Though not designed for military use, the Sayga weapons were also produced in versions suitable for security applications. A case in point is Sayga 20K. This is a folding-stock 20-bore version of the standard 410S shotgun. With its butt folded its length is 670mm (26.37in) and it has a pistol grip for an assault-rifle style of firing.

Above: Croatian soldiers on Christmas Day during the Yugoslavian civil war. The AKM rifle is still held at the ready; in this case two magazines have been taped together for rapid changing.

the SVD weapon. Keeping up to date, modified versions of the AK74 have appeared as well. These are known collectively as AI-74, and chambering has been for both 5.45mm and 5.56m cartridges, the latter being generally destined for export markets that use the NATO standard round.

SOUTH AFRICA

South Africa is two steps removed from the AK, having produced rifles based on the Israeli Galil. Like the Galil, the Vektor R4 was created as a replacement for the FAL (known as the R1 in South Africa). Whereas the Galil has a steel butt the R4 uses fibreglass-reinforced plastic to prevent heat build-up in the African sun, and the overall dimensions of the rifle are bigger to suit the generally larger South African physique.

Two subsequent versions of the R4 have emerged. The R5 is the R4's successor, and has been shortened in everything from the barrel to the gas system and also omits the bipod fitting of the R4. Taking the dimensions down further, the R6 is the rifle's compact version for use in confined areas. It is 565mm (22.24in) long in its butt-folded position.

YUGOSLAVIA/SERBIA

Space does not allow us to trawl through the amazing range of Yugoslavian AK copies or variants. After copying the AK47 in their Model 64 assault rifle, the company of Zavodi Crvena Zastava began to make submachine guns, other assault rifles and light machine guns around the AK model. Yet the design was never slavish. Even the original Model 64 had native features, including a longer barrel and a mechanical bolt hold-open device. In 7.62mm alone, four subsequent variants of the M64 were produced, the last being the M70A, before a new rifle – the M70B1 started its own line. From the early 1980s, the M80 assault rifle was produced in 5.45 x 45mm calibre, with rifling adapted for either the US M193 round or the Belgian SS109. This distinctive weapon visually appears to fall somewhere between an AK and the SVD, having a long barrel and a straight box magazine. Its gas-system has been enhanced over previous models. The latest version of the Yugoslavian assault rifles is the Model 85. Whereas the M80 is a fairly long weapon, the M85 has taken its inspiration from the Soviet AKS-74U and is a compact gun specifically for use by armoured crews.

Right: Soldiers of the Croatian army display an AKM variant on parade. Production of AK variants was extensive in the former Yugoslavia, including light machine guns and submachine guns.

AK VARIANTS

The variety of Yugoslavian light machine guns is equally advanced. The series began with the 7.62mm Model 65A, a heavy-barrelled, bipod-mounted version of the M64 rifle. This weapon, and those of the same type which followed, have a section of cooling ribs between the gas-port housing and the wooden fore-end, thus enabling them to be easily distinguished from other LMGs of Kalashnikov style. This feature disappears in the M82 light machine gun, based on the M80 assault rifle.

Variants of the AK47 will doubtless continue for many years yet. The most interesting issue is whether the AKs primary virtue of simplicity will disappear as markets compete with advanced features such as sophisticated burst modes and ultra-technical sighting accessories. Whether these features actually improve the soldier's survivability on the battlefield is another matter.

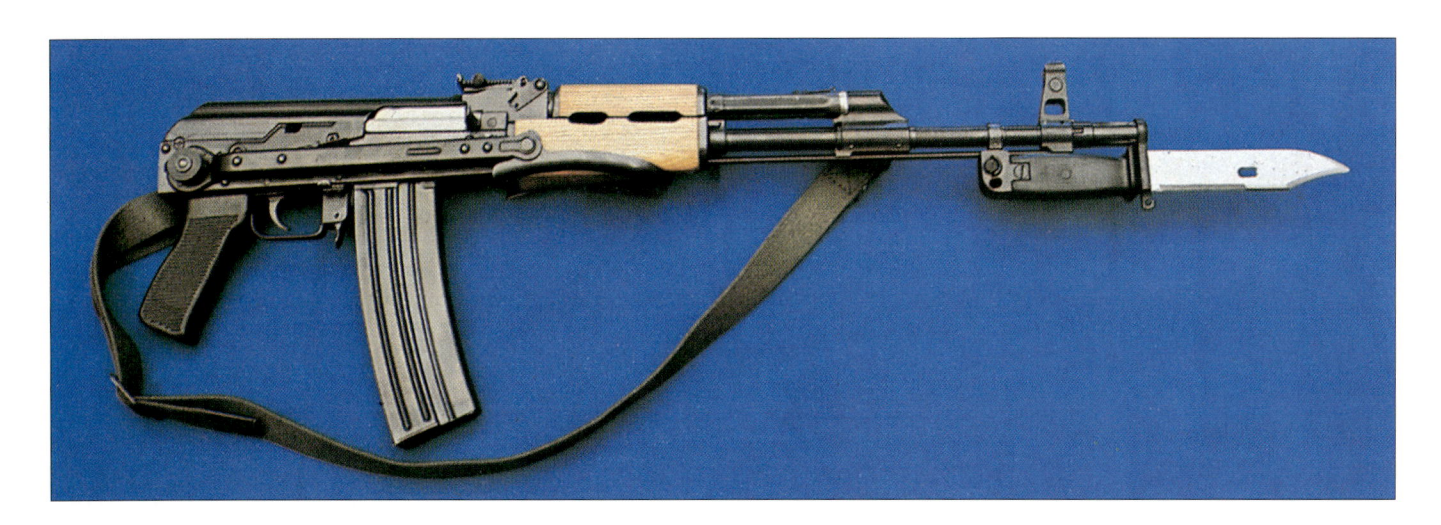

Below: The M80 was an AK variation manufactured in Yugoslavia/Serbia in 5.56mm calibre. The gun pictured here is actually the folding-stock version, the M80A, with fitted bayonet.

THE AK47

AK47 Specifications

MODEL	7.62MM AK47 ASSAULT RIFLE	7.62MM AKM ASSAULT RIFLE
Calibre	7.62 x 39mm M43 rimless	7.62 x 39mm M43 rimless
Operation	Gas-operation	Gas-operation
Length	9870mm (32.25in)	878mm (34.56in)
Weight	4.3kg (9.4lb)	3.85kg (8.4lb)
Barrel	R415mm (16.33in), four grooves, right hand	415mm (16.33in), four grooves, right hand
Magazine	Detachable 30-round box magazine	Detachable 30-round box magazine
Rate of fire	775rpm	600rpm
Muzzle velocity	710mps (2329fps)	710mps (2329fps)
Maximum range	800m (2624.6ft)	1000m (3280ft)

MODEL	7.62MM AK74 ASSAULT RIFLE	5.45MM AK-107 ASSAULT RIFLE
Calibre	5.45 x 39mm M74 rimless	5.45 x 39mm M74 rimless
Operation	Gas-operation	Gas-operation, counter-recoil system
Length	943mm (37.1in)	695mm (27.3in)
Weight	3.4kg (7.5lb)	3.6kg (7.2lb)
Barrel	415mm (16.33in), four grooves, right hand	415mm (16.33in), four grooves, right hand
Magazine	Detachable 30-round box magazine	Detachable 30-round box magazine
Rate of fire	600rpm	850-900rpm
Muzzle velocity	900mps (2952fps)	840mps (2755fps)
Maximum range	1000m (3280ft)	1000m (3280ft)

MODEL	AN-94 AKABAN	7.62MM RPK LIGHT MACHINE GUN
Calibre	5.45 x 39mm M74 rimless	7.62 x 39mm M43 rimless
Operation	Gas-operation	Gas-operation
Length	943mm (37.1in) stock extended; 728mm (28.6in) stockfolded	1040mm (40.9in)
Weight	3.85kg (8.47lb)	5kg (11.02lb) with bipod
Barrel	405mm (15.9in), four grooves, right hand	590mm (23.22in), four grooves, right hand
Magazine	Detachable 30-round box magazine	Detachable 30- or 40-round box magazine, 75-round drum
Rate of fire	1800 and 600rpm variable	600rpm
Muzzle velocity	n/a	735mps (2411fps)
Maximum range	n/a	1200m (3937ft)

MODEL	5.45MM RPK LIGHT MACHINE GUN	7.62MM SVD SNIPER RIFLE
Calibre	5.45 x 39mm M74 rimless	7.62 x 54R
Operation	Gas-operation	Gas-operation, semi-automatic
Length	1060mm (41.73in)	1220mm (48.03in)
Weight	5.64kg (12.43lb) with bipod	4.3kg (9.47lb), empty with PSO-1 magazine
Barrel	590mm (23.22in), four grooves, right hand	545mm (21.4in), four grooves, right hand
Magazine	Detachable 30-, 40- or 45-round box magazine	Detachable 10-round box magazine
Rate of fire	850rpm	N/A
Muzzle velocity	925mps (3034fps)	830mps (2723fps)
Maximum range	1000m (3280ft)	1300m (4265ft)

MODEL	YUGOSLAVIAN 7.62MM MODEL 64 ASSAULT RIFLE	REPUBLIC OF SOUTH AFRICA 5.56MM VEKTOR R4
Calibre	5.45 x 39mm M74 rimless	5.45 x 45mm
Operation	Gas-operation	Gas-operation
Length	1040mm (40.9in)	1005mm (39.56in) butt extended; 740mm (29.13in) butt folded
Weight	3.9kg (8.5lb)	4.3kg (9.4lb) without magazine
Barrel	500mm (19.68in), four grooves, right hand	460mm (18.11in), six grooves, right hand
Magazine	Detachable 30-round box magazine	Detachable 35-round box magazine
Rate of fire	775rpm	675rpm
Muzzle velocity	730mps (2395fps)	980mps (3215fps)
Maximum range	1000m (3280ft)	1000m (3280ft)

APPENDIX

MODEL	CHINESE 7.62MM TYPE 56 ASSAULT RIFLE	FINNISH 7.62MM MODEL 62 VALMET ASSAULT RIFLE
Calibre	7.62 x 39mm M43 rimless	7.62 x 39mm M43 rimless
Operation	Gas-operation	Gas-operation
Length	870mm (34.25in)	915mm (36in)
Weight	4.45kg (9.8lb)	4.0kg (8.8lb)
Barrel	415mm (16.33in), four grooves, right hand	420mm (16.53in), four grooves, right hand
Magazine	Detachable 30-round box magazine	Detachable 30-round box magazine
Rate of fire	775rpm	750rpm
Muzzle velocity	720mps (2362fps)	710mps (2329fps)
Maximum range	800m (2624ft)	1000m (3280ft)

MODEL	FINNISH 7.62MM MODEL 78 VALMET LIGHT MACHINE GUN	7.62MM AK-103 ASSAULT RIFLE
Calibre	7.62 x 51mm NATO rimless, 7.62 x 39mm M43, 5.56 x 45mm NATO	7.62 x 39mm M43 rimless
Operation	Gas-operation	Gas-operation
Length	1060mm (41.73in)	943mm (37.12in) butt extended; 700mm (27.5in) butt folded
Weight	4.7kg (10.36lb)	3.4kg (7.4lb)
Barrel	550mm (21.65in), four grooves, right hand	415mm (16.33in), four grooves, right hand
Magazine	Detachable 15- or 30-round box magazine	Detachable 30-round box magazine
Rate of fire	750rpm	775rpm
Muzzle velocity	720mps (2362fps) for M43 round	715mps (2345fps)
Maximum range	1000m (3280ft)	1000m (3280ft)

MODEL	5.45MM AKSU-74 SUBMACHINE GUN	5.56MM GALIL ARM
Calibre	5.45 x 39mm M74 rimless	5.56 x 45mm rimless
Operation	Gas-operation	Gas-operation
Length	675mm (26.57in) butt extended; 420mm (16.53in) butt folded	979mm (38.5in) butt extended; 742mm (29.2in) butt folded
Weight	2.7kg (5.9lb)	4.35kg (9.5lb)
Barrel	200mm (7.8in), four grooves, right hand	460mm (18.11in), six grooves, right hand
Magazine	Detachable 30-round box magazine	Detachable 12-, 25-, 35-, 50-round box magazine
Rate of fire	800rpm	650rpm
Muzzle velocity	735mps (2411fps)	980mps (3215fps)
Maximum range	500m (1640ft)	1000m (3280ft)

MODEL	POLISH 5.56MM KA-90 TANTAL ASSAULT RIFLE	POLISH 5.56MM KA-91 ONYX SUBMACHINE GUN
Calibre	5.56 x 45mm rimless	5.56 x 45mm rimless
Operation	Gas-operation	Gas-operation
Length	943mm (37.12in) butt extended; 742mm (29.21in) butt folded	720mm (28.34in) butt extended; 519mm (20.43in) butt folded
Weight	3.4kg (7.49lb)	2.9kg (6.3lb)
Barrel	423mm (16.65in), four grooves, right hand	207mm (8.14in), four grooves, right hand
Magazine	Detachable 30-round box magazine	Detachable 30-round box magazine
Rate of fire	700rpm	700rpm
Muzzle velocity	900mps (2952fps)	710mps (2329fps)
Maximum range	800m (2624ft)	400m (1312ft)

MODEL	HUNGARIAN 5.56MM NGM ASSAULT RIFLE	ROMANIAN 5.45MM KA-90 AI-74 ASSAULT RIFLE
Calibre	5.56 x 45mm rimless	5.45 x 39mm M74
Operation	Gas-operation	Gas-operation
Length	979mm (38.54in) butt extended; 742mm (29.21in) butt folded	940mm (37in)
Weight	4.35kg (9.5lb)	3.4kg (7.49lb)
Barrel	460mm (18.11in), six grooves, right hand	415mm (16.33in), four grooves, right hand
Magazine	Detachable 12-, 25-, 35- or 50-round box magazine	Detachable 30-round box magazine
Rate of fire	650rpm	700rpm
Muzzle velocity	980mps (3215fps)	880mps (2887fps)
Maximum range	800m (2624ft)	800m (2624ft)

Distinctions between the AK47 and AKM

FEATURE	AK47	AKM
Furniture	Wooden butt and fore-end; pistol grips of laminated plastic	All parts laminated wood, plastic or nylon
Gas piston tube	Four holes on each side for gas venting	Two semi-circular cut-outs
Rearsight	Graduated to 800m	Graduated to 1000m
Mainspring guide	Steel rod	Sometimes constructed of two wires
Receiver body	From 1951 machined from solid steel block	Stamped steel with indentations just over the magazine housing and bolt locking recesses riveted inside
Receiver cover	Smooth finish	Can feature three vertical ridges
Bolt carrier	Natural steel or chrome finish	Parkerised finish
Rate reducing mechanism	None	Trigger delay mechanism fitted
Bayonet lug	Generally not fitted	Usually fitted

The AN-94 'Abakan'

The replacement for the AK rifles in Russia, reportedly much to the chagrin and protests of Kalashnikov himself, is the AN-94 Abakan (the codename for the trials which took place in the early 1990s to look for an AK replacement). Whereas the AK exploited simplicity, the AN-94 is a very sophisticated weapon indeed. The calibre remains the same as the AK74 – 5.45 x 39mm – but the operating system is very different. The AN-94's operation is called blow-back shifted pulse, effectively a mixture of gas- and recoil-operation. This very complex system involves the barrel and receiver assembly recoiling upon firing during which time the bolt and bolt carrier have actually cycled twice before the user feels the recoil of the two shots (this is assuming that the user has selected full-automatic fire or the AN-94's distinctive two-round burst). Furthermore, a cable and pulley feed system actually half load each round even while the bolt and bolt carrier are moving backwards, thus giving the two-round burst an enormous cyclical rate of 1800rpm (on full-auto the first two rounds are fired at this rate before dropping to 600rpm). The result is that two shots are felt as one recoil pulse after both rounds have left the muzzle, and the accuracy gained through this system is considerable.

The concept of the AN-94 is a strong one, but the system of operation is involved. It is now in production though currently it is only being delivered to Russian Spetsnaz soldiers and Belarus is also receiving quantities of the weapon.

Calibre	5.45 x 39mm M74
Operation	Blow-back shifted pulse
Length	943mm (37.1in) stock extended; 728mm (28.6in) stock folded
Weight	3.85kg (8.47lb) empty, without magazine
Barrel	405mm (15.9in), four grooves, right hand
Magazine	Detachable 30-round box magazine
Rate of fire	Variable 1800 and 600rpm
Muzzle velocity	N/A
Maximum range	N/A

Index

Afghanistan
    Mujahideen 66-7, *66*
    Soviet occupation *48-9*, 61, *64*, 66-7
African National Congress 49
AGS 17 grenade launcher *64*
AIM [Romania] *87*, 89
AK47 *52-3*, *58*, *64*, *83*
    accuracy 37, 42
    arms trade 56-8
    derivatives 31
    kill probability 53
    licensed manufacture 57
    production numbers 31, 54
    prototypes 19
    reliability 37, 42, 45-7, 54, 64
    status symbol 49
    Type I 23-5
    Type II *22*, 26
    Type III 26-7
AK74 31, *56*, *64*, *68-9*
    accuracy 43, 53, 70
    development 71
    furniture 71-2
    kill probability 53, 70
    muzzle brake 70, 71
    recoil 42-3, 53, 71
    reliability 71
AK101 72
AK102 submachine-gun 76
AK103 31, 72, *73*
AK104 submachine gun 31, 75-6
AK105 submachine-gun 76
AK107 72, 74
AK108 72, 74
AKB/AKB-1 74
AKK [Bulgaria] 82
AKM *22*, *28*, *39*
    accessories 30-31
    accuracy 52-3
    design 27, 29
    recoil 42, 52
    silencers 43, 45
AKM-63 [Hungary] 84
AKMS 29
AKMS-U submachine-gun 75
AKS47 25, *32-3*
AKS74 25, *72*
AKS74U submachine gun *73*, 74, 76
AKS74UN submachine gun 76
AKS74Y submachine gun 76

AL7 74
Al Quds machine gun [Iraq] 86
Albania 56, 60-61
AMD-65 [Hungary] 84, 86
ammunition
    full power 8-9, *8*, 70
    impact 50, *50*, 52
    intermediate 7, *8*, 14, 15, 70
    lethality 50, 52, 70
    production standards 45, 46
AN94 74
arms trade
    Africa 58, *60*, 62
    Asia 61-2
    Europe 58, 60-61
    illegal 54, 58, 67
    Latin America 62
    Russia officers 60
automatic mode 23, 39, 42
    accuracy 37
    climb *27*
    rates 29, 42
AVT40 rifle 19

barrels 25
bayonets, wire-cutting 30-31, *39*
Bizon submachine-gun 76-7
blow-back 17
blow-back operation 30
Bulgaria 57, 82

cartridges 7-8, 11, 14
China *see* Type 56
Chinese Army *54*
Chinese Navy *55*
Croatian Army *56*, *91*
Cuban Army *39*, *62*

date stamps 25, 26
Degtyarev, V.A. 9, 16
Dragunov, Alexey 76, 78

East German [GDR] Army *20-21*, *43*
East Germany 57, 84
Egypt 83
Egyptian Army *23*, *65*
ejection 47, 71
Encounter Battles 36-7
Eritrea *60*, *81*
Ethiopia 62
extraction 47

Federov, 6.5mm Avtomat 13-14
Federov, Vladimir Grigorevich 9, 13
field stripping *24*, *43*, 45
Finland 83-4
FN FAL 65
FPK sniper rifle [Romania] 89-90
furniture
    AK47 25, 26
    AK74 71-2
    AKM 29

Galil ARM [Israel] 66, 86-8, *88-9*
gas cylinder operation 22, 30
German Army *10*
Grenada *59*, *61*
grenade launchers 30, *72*, *79*
Guinea *60*

hand grenades 46
hit rates 42
Hungary 57, 84, 86

image intensifier sights 30, 41
Iraq 49, 86
Israel 65-6, 86-7

KA-88 Tantal [Poland] 88
KA-89 Onyx submachine-gun [Poland] 88
KA-96 Beryl [Poland] 89
Kalashnikov, Mikhail Timofeyevich 17
    awards 33
    biography 15-16
    Federov's influence 13
    prototype AK47 16-19
    self-loading carbine 17-18
Kalashnikov, Viktor 76, 78
Kravchenko, Zhena 16
Kurz round 7.92x33mm 14

Liberia 62

M16A1
    lethality 50, 52
    reliability 54, 61, 64
    sights 39, 41
M35 7.75/7.62 cartridge 14
M43 [M1943] ammunition 13, 16-17, 32-3, 50
    BZ armour-piercing 33

PS 32-3
T-45 tracer 33
Z incendiary 33
M60 [Finland] 83
M62 [Finland] 83-4
M74 ammunition 52, 70-71
M80 [Yugoslavia] 90-91, *91*
M85 [Yugoslavia] 91
M95 [Finland] 84
M1891 ammunition 9
machine guns 77-79
magazines
    capacity 37-8, *43*
    design 25
    feed problems 46-7
    loading 38-9
    storing 38
Makarov PM pistol 46
manufacture
    machining 26
    pressing and stamping 24
Mauser *10*
Meiji 6.5mm 30 cartridge 13
MG42 machine gun 77
Misr [Egypt] 83
MKb35 14
Model 3 [Armenia] 81
Mosin-Nagant
    7.62mm rifles *9*, *12*, 36
    7.62x54R cartridges 9
MP43/MP44/StG44 13, 14-15
MPi-K series [East Germany] 84
muzzles
    AK47 *27*
    AK74 70
    AKM *27*

NGM881 [Hungary] 86
Nigeria *83*
North Korea [PRK] 57, 87-8
Northern Ireland 49, 61

Oman, Dhofari guerrillas *26*

Pakistan, US arms 61
pistols 46
PMK series [Poland] *31*, 88
Poland 88-9
Polish Army *31*, *40*, *47*, *86*
PPD34/38/40 submachine guns 16
PPS41 submachine gun 16, 36

PPS43 submachine gun 15, 16, 36
PPSh41 submachine gun 6-7, 11, 12-13, 25
production
    Type I 23-4
    Type II 26
proof marks 25, 26
PU-1/PU-2/PU-21 machine guns 78-9

R4/R5/R6 Vektor [South Africa] 90
Radom-Hunter sniper rifle 77
RDG-5 hand grenade 46
receivers
    AK47 24-5, 26, 27
    AKM 29
recoil
    AK47 42-3, 52
    AK74 42-3, 53, 71
recoil operation 30
reliability
    AK47 37, 42, 45-7, 53-4
    AK74 71
rifles, barrel length 8-9
RKG3M anti-tank grenade 46
Romania 57, 89-90
Romanian Army 29, 32, 34-5
rotating-bolt action 17

gas operated 22-3, 46
RPD 29
RPK machine gun 30, 37, 67, 77-8, 78-9, 86
RPK74 machine gun 76
RPKS machine gun 78
RPKS74 series machine guns 78
Rukavashnikov, Nikolay 11

Samoylov, Ivan 79
Sayga shotguns 31, 81, 89
semi-automatic mode 23, 39, 41-2
Serbian Army 28
serial numbers 25, 26
Shpagin, Georgi 16
sights
    AK47 25, 39, 41
    AKM 29, 30
    image intensifying 30, 41
    optical 81
    thermal imaging 30, 41
silencers 30, 43, 45, 76
Simonov, Sergey 9, 11
Simonov SKS carbine 16, 18
Six-day War 65-6
sniper rifles 79-81
South Africa 58, 90

Soviet Army
    Afghanistan 48-9, 61, 64, 66-7
    AK47 36-7
    tactics 35-7
Soviet naval infantry 68-9, 71
Soviet tanks
    BMP-2 37
    T34 14
    T54 38
Stechkin APS pistol 46
submachine-guns 16, 75-7
SVD sniper rifle 31, 67, 79-81, 80-81
SVT38 automatic rifle 11, 17
SVT40 automatic rifle 11, 17, 19
SVT40 rifle 18
Syrian Army 87

Tabuk [Iraq] 85, 86
thermal imaging sights 30, 41, 76
Tokarev, automatic rifles 9, 11
Tokarev, Fedor 9, 11
training, laser beams 57
trench warfare 8
trigger action 22, 39
    automatic fire 29, 39
    semi-automatic 23, 39
Type 56 [China] 54, 56, 80

manufacture 62, 82
trade in 56, 61
variations 82-3
Type 58 [North Korea] 87-8
Type 68 [North Korea] 88
Type 81 [China] 83
Type 86 [China] 83

UNITA army 80
US Army
    AK47 59, 62, 82
    Rangers 61, 62
    Special Forces 51

Vietnam War 56, 61, 62, 63-5, 63

Yugoslavia 57, 90-91

Zaytsev, Aleksandr 19

Picture Credits

Jkt (front): Art work: **Aerospace Publishing**; Photographs: **TRH Pictures**
Jkt (back): **Tim Ripley**.

Ian V. Hogg: 8, 15, 41, 42, 43 (t), 50, 74, 77, 86, 87 (t), 91 (t).

Tim Ripley: 2-3, 20-21, 28, 29, 31, 32, 34-35, 40, 44, 47.

Novosti: 17.

TRH Pictures: 6-7 (US National Archives), 9, 10 (US National Archives), 11, 12 (t), 13 (r), 14, 16, 19, 22 (S. Bull), 24 (S. Bull), 25, 27 (both) (S. Bull), 30, 37 (Richard Stickland), 38, 43 (b), 48-49, 51 (US Army), 54, 55, 56 (J P Husson), 57, 58, 59 (US Dept. of Defense), 60 (both), 61 (US Dept. of Defense), 62 (US Dept. of Defense), 64, 65, 66, 67, 68-69, 70, 71(TASS), 72, 73 (both), 75, 76 (G D Taylor), 79 (NATO), 80, 81, 82 (US Dept. of Defense), 84 (US Dept. of Defense / USN), 85 (USN), 87 (b) (US Dept. of Defense), 90 (J P Husson), 91 (b) (J P Husson).

Artworks:

Aerospace Publishing: 12-13, 32-33, 52-53, 78-79, 80-81, 88-89.
De Agostini UK: 18, 23, 26, 36, 39, 63, 83.